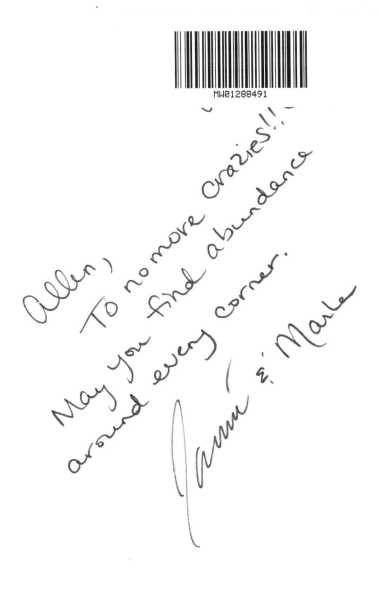

Allen)
To no more Crazies!!
May you find abundance
around every corner.

Jamie & Marle

How Men Make Women Crazy

(and Vice Versa): Ending the Madness

JAMI AND MARLA KELLER

iUniverse, Inc.
New York   Bloomington

iUniverse books may be ordered through booksellers or by contacting:

iUniverse
1663 Liberty Drive
Bloomington, IN 47403
www.iuniverse.com
1-800-Authors (1-800-288-4677)

ISBN: 978-1-4502-6088-6 (sc)
ISBN: 978-1-4502-6087-9 (ebook)

Printed in the United States of America

iUniverse rev. date: 11/22/2010

For Kayla and Ariel and your future husbands!
Your beauty and intuition inspire us every day. You make us desire to be
better spouses, lovers, friends, parents and most of all better followers of
the Trinitarian life. You CAN have it all.

CONTENTS

ACKNOWLEDGMENTS

HOW MEN MAKE WOMEN CRAZY! The title is perfect and the fun we had writing was surprising! Once again we were reminded, that it takes a team. Our first THANK YOU goes to Lesley Dick. We were blessed that the Internet could take our book to Switzerland while she was there and back to us with hard questions like "what are you trying to say?" Dr. Shawn States: Your skepticism makes our book stronger, so THANK YOU! For Jennifer who wanted us to put more of the "gory details" into the book for ratings. =) You are beauty and intuition personified!! For all of you who allowed us to use parts of your story THANK YOU! Chanel, your perspectives made us think a little harder. THANK YOU! And THANK YOU to Jarod and Kelly who let us use their story with their actual names attached to it—you guys are amazing, and we are so proud of you and the good work you have done in your marriage! Keep it up!!

There are too many to list here, but you know who you are and your support is so appreciated and we thank God for each of you every day. THANK YOU!

Much love to each of you,
Marla and Jami

The Beginning of the Ending of Craziness

In 2005 we met Gina at a wine bar. She was cheerfully serving and we were looking for a way to get to know the community. We gave her a brochure about our Couples Coaching. She mentioned that she would tell her twin sister and hopefully Jennifer would call. Jennifer called soon after. She told us, "I feel like I am going CRAZY! I keep telling my husband that I feel something is wrong and he keeps telling me everything is fine."

We had heard ladies tell us this before, but Jennifer put a finer point on it. She was willing to settle for her disconnected marriage if we would tell her that was a good idea for her. But she just felt like there was so much more to marriage, and that they could be so much more connected. She knew great intimacy was there for them but obviously there was some sort of block. She was willing to consider herself the problem, but something about him was bothering her. She could not get him to share and he seemed distracted. Their adorable baby girl had added some welcomed stress into their life. But she knew he was slipping away.

Jennifer's story is all too often the case. Intuition interrupted. She warned her husband that something was wrong all along the way, and he put her off. We do not blame men in this book; we have been involved in too many relationships to think that one partner is to blame. What we hope to point out is how a man can choose strength and integrity, and how a woman can thrive in her intuition and beauty and stop those feelings of "going CRAZY".[1]

Also it is very important to say that any one person can bring a relationship to a place of choice for intimacy. We have seen 44 year marriages that were complete misery for one partner turn around and be a joyful connection with new depths of respect and love. It is not complicated, but it is work. This work is more than worth it!

---

[1] Stasi and John Eldredge have written a book called *Captivating* that addresses this concept more fully. We highly recommend it.

SECTION ONE

Listen & Express Feelings

ONE
Can You Feel?

*"Personally, I experience the greatest degree of pleasure in having contact with works of art. They furnish me with happy **feelings** of an intensity such as I cannot derive from other realms."*

Albert Einstein

"Relationships are the greatest work of art in our lives!"

Jami and Marla Keller

Fun, successful loan officer meets sexy grade school teacher. They both have many friends and they like to party. The scene is less and less fun for them, with the drinking and drama of college grad's continued "adolescence" obviously not meeting their needs. They make a major decision. They move away from the California town that has all the party social circles and move in together. The hope is that the new surroundings and the "upgrading" of their commitment to each other will stop the cycle of dirty fighting and making up that is common to their daily and weekly pattern. It only got worse.

Our Coaching process begins with a focus not on the story, but on feelings. While each persons' story is very important and can have a strong impact on them and those near them, without feelings stories would be pointless. An important thing to remember is that "good", "okay" and "fine" are not feelings, but descriptions—

part of a story that describes what happened but completely leaves out real feelings.

The first question is "Can you feel?" Given a specific instance such as "when you saw that your husband left to play with his friends for the one free afternoon you could have had together" can you give three feelings? If there is any difficulty expressing core feelings at this moment, one has to ask, **"What is it that is keeping you from being connected with your feelings and expressing them healthfully?"** It is a very important question. We could all benefit from asking ourselves this on a regular basis. There are many stressors that limit our ability to feel, and we will explore many aspects of this, but first how well do you recognize your feelings? Let's dig deep: the **core feelings** we have to be able to recognize are **fear and rejection, and peace and love.**

The most important truth about feelings is there are no "bad" feelings. One feeling people often consider "bad" is anger. Not only is anger not bad, it is something you need to feel and express healthfully so as not to create more pain in your life from stuffing it.

Anger is the result of your core fear being tapped. And having anger is an important sign that something is wrong. Emotions give us the energy to move. Dealing with anger is a vital part of relationships. Anger should be welcomed as a topic for action in all relationships, and should not be feared or hidden.

According to research, and our personal experience, everyone's core fear is the fear of *rejection*.[1] Beyond this, when conflict occurs most women's core fear is *abandonment* and most men's core fear is the *fear of being controlled*. (This is what we call the Key-Dagger and will discuss in detail in the section of *Vision Future Intimacy.*)

Being aware of feelings takes practice. In chapter seven we detail our recommended daily focused journal. We have found that when you focus daily on being aware of feelings during the journaling time, expressing them healthfully comes much easier. In order to change, we must do things differently. We do not ask people to do this forever, but it can be life-changing even if it's just done for six weeks. We know this can sound daunting, but isn't ten minutes a day worth improving your personal satisfaction in relationships?

When Marla and I coached Jarod and Kelly (some of the names in this book have been changed for confidentiality), we found that her feeling abandoned by all the men before him, including her father, was compounded by having no wedding date. Her expressing this would leave Jarod feeling inadequate and frustrated, particularly when Kelly didn't express real feelings just kept saying the same thing over and over again, louder and louder trying desperately to get Jarod to understand her. This of course leads to what we call the "sick-play". Sick-plays come up over and over again in our relationship coaching. Let us illustrate with a composite of several relationships. See if some part of this is familiar to you.

Marvin and Eve are both in their second marriage where they have fallen madly in love. They get to experience freedom in their relationship on the weekends that the children from the first marriages are with their exes. Eve has financial issues and the ex-husband is very good at not paying and/or hiding money, and is terribly manipulative about how custody is shared and is always breaking boundaries.

There are some real problems with the ex and Eve has some huge justification for being screaming mad about how the transactions happen. So here comes the shining knight to rescue. Marvin is "Mr. Marvelous". He brings to the relationship his good job and house equity, and moves across the state so the kids won't have to move schools. Because he provides financially for Eve and her children, that form of control is effectively taken away from Mr. Wrong. Then in a genius move Mr. Marvelous takes over the negotiation of the kid's visits with their dad from Eve. It makes sense, and it alleviates all that time wasted from feeling abused and angry over having to look at and listen to Mr. Wrong.

Suddenly all of Eve's drama is gone. The children have adjusted, and even if they don't totally love Marvin they at least appreciate his stabilizing influence. The chaos is gone! Now there is a giant empty spot where "Chaos" dwelt and suddenly being quiet with herself becomes difficult. Not surprisingly, issues of abuse between she and her Dad begin to reveal themselves.

Suddenly her fundamental issues with men become more evident to the observer and totally overwhelming to her. Eve's fractured childhood relationship with her father began to fracture her ability to be intuitive and crushed the belief that she was beautiful. It also created in her the feeling that she must just be crazy, and she may never be happy.

All of a sudden Marvin is boring and predictable to Eve. Marvelous Marvin becomes Mundane Marvin and other men's advances become very enticing. His issues (or past issues) with pornography, or previous women, are suddenly issues that become overwhelming. Her need for sex with Marvin decreases, or is repulsive and unsatisfying, and her need for emotional validation from other men increases.

She does not consciously realize why she puts herself in positions to flirt with disaster, i.e., shopping and spending too much, emotionally bonding with "dangerous" men, taking on way too much at work, rescuing other family members, and abandoning or over-bonding with the children. Marvin's strength and integrity are severely challenged.

Marvin is at first very validated by the obvious miracle he has worked. As Eve slips sideways, and further from him emotionally and sexually, he becomes aware of the distance but has too much at stake to set reasonable boundaries with her. He denies the obvious and makes excuses for the "new drama" that creeps in to their life together. His issues of pornography and alcohol use, or workaholism, begin again and there is a distance between him and his old support system. Doubt and passivity dominate his new family life so he sinks himself into his addictions that have plagued him throughout his life, and his ability to have true intimacy is now more out of reach than ever. Eve's beauty and intuition are fractured more deeply because his deception and passivity.

The children's behavior responds directly to Eve and Marvin's meltdown. Grades slip; trouble with the neighbor's turns into trouble with the law. Rejection of the new parent is at first passive-aggressive and spurs the Cinderella syndrome (Eve's step-children are treated as slaves as opposed to being treated as her own children). Suddenly, fairness is always an issue and the children are too much a focus of this relationship. The honeymoon is over and now it is time to face the issues or fail again with higher consequences than last time.

There are usually huge hidden agendas. A relationship may also be more complicated by complex financial issues resulting from the hiding of addictions which are expensive in more ways than one. But if these are made into the focus the marriage usually fails.

In our coaching process we turn away from the sick-play by recognizing that most of what is currently happening is really about fear of repeating a past hurt. We don't even have to worry about what those are, we know that it is fundamentally fear of abandonment or fear of control. So we focus on what really works: Forgiveness.

Does this sound familiar or look like where you are heading? Any one of these things a person could handle. You can see your way through a problem with a child when you are connected with your spouse. There is a voice of reason when confronted with heavy flirting outside the marriage by itself. We usually don't get hung up on the chains of pornography overnight. But a woman's intuition is destroyed by the fear placed in her heart from the men in her life beginning in childhood: the fear of infidelity and the fear of rejection. This is the dagger that has been plunged into the keyhole of her heart that began with her father's abandonment and/or control.

How does this happen? How did this sick-play get started? The attack on this relationship started generations ago. Also, research has shown that the emotional life of the fetus begins at 4 months gestation, and this is another place where the attack on your security begins. What the mother feels while her child is in the womb is what the child experiences. *And* new research is showing that the father's feelings, which have until recently been disregarded, have a significant impact on the unborn child's emotions. ". . . [L]atest studies indicate that . . . how a man feels about his wife and unborn child is one of the single most important factors in determining the success of the pregnancy."[2]

The issues of your great-grandparents land in your lap and are the reason why your parents chose each other and why you chose the significant partners you have chosen. We don't think it is vital to know what all the issues were, though some people find this very interesting, and it is not necessarily healing just to identify a childhood pain without taking the steps toward healing. What *is* healing is to forgive, and this comes later in this book.

We find the illustration of war to be very helpful. It is obvious to us that there is a war over your heart and the hearts of your children, or anyone you are connected to. This is why movies like

Ever After, The Wizard of Oz and *The Lord of the Ring* are so popular. They describe a journey from our weakness to strength, sickness to health and the battle over lies and deception that plague us. They remind us that we are in a great story and that the first thing we must do to resolve our conflict is face the truth and TELL THE TRUTH.[3]

Why is telling the truth about our feelings so hard? Obviously there is the fear of pain when we share our core feelings. But also there is a habit formed after that pain. Too often we develop the habit of not feeling our feelings because it might hurt too much. We address this in a program that follows the movie "Ever After". We follow Drew Barrymore as Cinderella and her prince dance a web of half truths and find out how we do these things in our lives in "Forever After" available at Inviteinc.org.

Our problems with relationships begin with mistrust as well as our inability to identify how we truly feel. How do you feel right now? Can you name three core feelings? Really core? While your story is epic no matter who you are, your feelings are absolutely necessary for your healing journey. You are designed to be so much more than someone who hides their feelings. Especially if you hide them so well you can't find them.

The *Feeling Wheel* on the following page helps to identify what is going on inside of you:

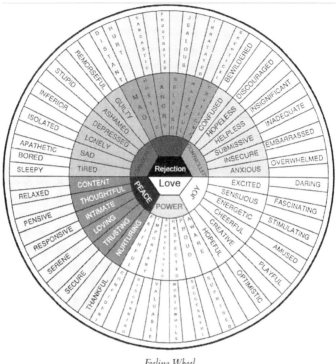

Feeling Wheel

Notice the hub of the wheel. The eight feelings that make up the core of what we feel are very important to be aware of. Are you able to feel each one distinctly? This is where the journaling can be very effective.

Feelings are so important because they unlock generations of crap and release us from the sick-play. The sick-play in your relationship can be illustrated by holding out your hand palm up and laying flat on the table, your partner doing the same with the opposite hand. Then rotate your hands from pinky to thumb. Each finger interlocking with your partners like a sprocket illustrates the issues you both bring to the table. It is clear to us from observation that they are not the same issues but matching issues. When your issues are played out you hit thumbs and that represents your fights. We do this over and over again until we choose to express our deepest feelings, secrets and dreams to each other, therefore healing our relationship and making whole and holy our lives together.

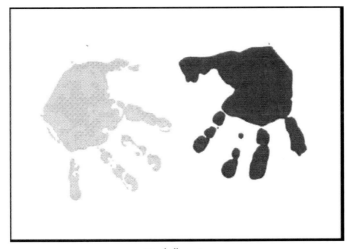

Hand Illustration

Make no mistake, your partner was chosen by you because you are very close to the same level of intelligence and you bring the KEY-DAGGER to your partners' heart. The Key to unlock more love and connection than you ever thought possible, and the Dagger to cut them down at the core, creating scars and pain that are very difficult but so necessary to forgive and overcome.

A sick-play is what happens when you feel unheard, either because you are not expressing your feelings well—expecting your significant other to "heart read" or tell you, or dropping hints hoping that they will figure it out, or blaming, or many other self-defeating techniques that you and I can be very skilled at—or not expressing them at all.

This cycle is different for us all, but very predictable. If we step back it looks like each of us is on a stage in the shape of circle. Check out the diagram below to better understand this concept. **a)** The two circles are touching and at that point we are standing close to each other, and this is the place where we are hugging and being happy. **b)** Then each of us takes one step clockwise as tension builds, subtle at first, then as we take further steps, **c)** we start throwing daggers at each other, until we are throwing all we have at the person we love the most. **d)** A few more steps to cool off, then we make up and kiss and make up, enjoying a "honeymoon" until we take those tension building steps and sharpen our daggers. The time it takes to make the circle around the stage depends on the people involved, and this might not be an obvious cycle. We all can be very passive or even neglectful.

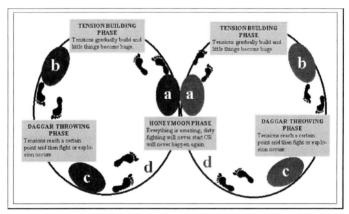

Fight Cycle

Often this cycle will increase in speed and bring us to a crisis point. This does not bring resolution, but often then changes the "rules" we follow as we continue on our "sick-play" until we find a safe way to relate our feelings to each other. The new "rules" will often slow the cycle for a time, but most of the time this cycle increases in pace with either more violence (control) or more isolation (abandonment) occurring at each turn of the stage.

Here lies the complication!

Do you remember the rules of engaging with the opposite sex changing back and forth when you were in grade school? Picture yourself on the playground in 3rd grade. First the boy hits the girl on the shoulder or calls her a name—in fun but with just enough "hostile humor" to get her attention—then he runs. She runs after him until she tires of this game and she stops. In effect, she changes the rules. He notices she is not chasing anymore and then the sick-play starts again. Get the point?

The control-abandonment game switches, and there are three combinations for each person (control, abandon or love) making nine combinations for a couple. (Trust us for now, it's a math thing but stay focused). This is why it can be tricky to evaluate what stage you are in at a given moment, because we tend to justify ourselves and blame the other. For the sake of love allow yourself to let it be what it is and stop with the blame/justification even of yourself because that story just won't work for anyone.

By recognizing the sick-play, the hurt of abandonment and control issues, as well as feeling worthy of love and applying healthy communication, Jarod and Kelly were able to embrace the fundamental agreements below that make all the difference in long term relationships.

- **First Best Agreement**

First, if we want to attain any intimacy we must agree that each of us has feelings and each of us has every right to express those feelings. The other person is not responsible for our feelings, but must be able to hear and understand those feelings. When you do this you are not necessarily agreeing with the reasons for those feelings, you are simply allowing them to feel their feelings.

- **Second Best Agreement**

The second agreement is to forgive each other, and the others that have hurt us. Forgiveness is addressed in the second section of this book, but most critically for Jarod and Kelly who had done so much "dirty fighting" they had to say to each other specifically what hurt, and choose to forgive each other. This process is almost always difficult because we are so good a justifying our daggers and we can become very attached to our stories and this can mask our feelings. Still Jarod and Kelly were able to do this.

- **Third Best Agreement**

Finally for a lasting relationship a couple must have a commitment to healthy community. In this day and age this means a social group that is connected and accountable to each other without becoming toxic with control. This can be done several ways and with a combination of groups, but must include shared values, mentoring, and a supportive environment. One place you can find this is in a twelve step program called *Recovering Couples Anonymous*.[4] This group was profound for us and we talk more about it in our book *Our Real Journey*.

Happily, Jarod and Kelly discovered how important these agreements are, and as a result they were able to totally change the negative impacts of the hurt in their lives, get off that sick-play stage, and start on a path of intimacy. This brought them to a healthy marriage, getting out of debt, and having their first baby. That was made possible because their commitment to these simple steps: sharing feelings, agreeing to forgive, and committing to community. These things have made all the difference in their lives today.

---

[1] Rejection Research: Fotti et al. *2006*; Loeber and Stouthamerloeber *1986*; Parker and Asher *1987*.

[2] *Pre-Parenting* by Dr. Thomas Verney

[3] We appreciate the mentorship of our relationship with each other through the books of John and Stasi Eldredge. Here are a few: *Captivating, The Way of the Wild Heart, Sacred Romance* and *Waking the Dead*.

[4] Go to http://www.recovering-couples.org/ for more information.

TWO

Rules About Feelings

"The first rule of business is: Do other men for they would do you."

Charles Dickens

*"All good business is built on high quality relationships
and business rules do not apply."*

Jami and Marla

As a child I (Marla) was the pleaser, the fixer, the one who made everyone laugh. As long as I was making everyone else in my family "okay", I was okay. But as soon as I began my healing journey and started to take care of my feelings, I immediately became the enemy. I was told that I had no right to feel the way that I did, and that if I didn't respond the way they wanted me to they really didn't want me as part of their family. It was very painful, and yet the most freeing thing I had experienced up to that point in my life. I say "freeing" because I had been held captive to my inability to be me; to experience life as Marla, and not who everyone around me wanted Marla to be.

Interestingly, Jami had a similar experience. He was often told to "stop crying or I'll give you something to cry about". He came to believe that he had no right to feel, and shut down his feelings completely. By the time he checked himself in to rehab, he had stifled his feelings so much that when his ability to feel was turned back on he actually felt nauseous, like he might be getting the flu.

In our recovery, we learned not only the importance of feelings, but that there are some hard, fast rules about feelings that cannot be ignored. Our relationship would not have recovered had we not learned these rules and stuck with them. Here they are:

- **<u>Rule #1</u> Feelings are real and factual. No one can disagree with your feelings or tell you that what you are feeling isn't real. And you have no right to discount someone else's feelings or make someone else responsible for your feelings.**

Something I had the hardest time accepting was that Jami wasn't responsible for my feelings. I would be angry and hurt for the thousandth time about Jami's infidelity and would lash out and scream, "You make me so angry!" He would look at me patiently and gently (most of the time) and say the most exasperating thing . . . "I am not responsible for your feelings." Ugghhhhh! But he was absolutely correct. I am the only person responsible for my feelings. I can choose to be angry or peaceful or frustrated, etc., but these are my feelings and are not Jami's responsibility. BUT . . .

. . . because Jami loves and respects me, he can choose to modify behaviors that hurt me. This is his choice and cannot be forced. I eventually learned to be responsible for my feelings, and that has made a huge difference in my reactions to pain. Caring for each other is about listening and connecting, not changing who we are but growing together into a much bigger story of love.

When you're in a relationship, being able to allow the other person their feelings without discounting them or trying to fix them will create a beautiful dynamic. The dagger that is so easily used to stab the other person in the heart becomes the key that unlocks true love and intimacy.

- **<u>Rule #2</u> There are no "bad" feelings.**

Even though we live in a society that says that anger or depression or jealousy is bad, there are no bad feelings. Every feeling is just that – a feeling. But what we do with our feelings can be bad, like lashing out with mean and untrue words during a fight because we know exactly what buttons to push and what things to say to hurt the other person the deepest.

So, as we said before, it is okay to feel angry, but be careful how you express that anger. The very best way to let that anger go is to journal those feelings to the Higher Power. You may even journal the feelings and then burn it so that there is a visual release. For more ways to express feelings appropriately through journaling, letter-writing, as well as talking, check out the chapters on *Check-In*, *Journaling* and *Letter Writing*. Also, to begin evaluating what you are feeling more deeply, refer back to the *Feeling Wheel* on page 16.

- **<u>Rule #3</u> You are allowed to have two or more contradictory feelings at the same time.**

It is not only possible, but probable that you love someone but are angry at them at the same time. It is also possible to be excited about a new position at work, but be fearful because of what changes and conflicts that might create in your life. You may feel peaceful about your forgiveness of your father, but still feel frustrated with him. One feeling does not rule out the other one that appears to contradict the first. The most important thing is that you are aware of each feeling and are able to process them appropriately.

- <u>Rule #4</u> Painful feelings will become potent when we do not identify them or express them.

Keeping painful feelings below the surface and not expressing them will be felt by others even when you don't realize it. People around you know how you feel even when you don't say a word. Have you ever walked into a room where someone was angry, and you could just feel that anger seething and dripping down the walls? It's because we all exude pheromones[1] that create a knowledge of something before it is even expressed.

Feelings that are not expressed or identified because of denial or the need to stuff them so far down because of the fear of feeling pain, and they turn into oozing barrels of toxic crap that will end up exploding somehow. What does that look like? Well, you will eventually come to your breaking point and explode in anger, or your body will absorb it and you will end up getting sick. There's a great saying about this – "You either become better or bitter." Bitterness only leads to a very negative end. So, learn to identify and express your feelings or they may end up killing you in the end.

---

[1] Pheromones are an agent secreted by an individual that produces a change in the sexual or social behavior of another individual of the same species; a volatile hormone that acts as a behavior-altering agent. – *www.medicinenet.com.*

THREE

How to Recognize Feelings

"Miracles are a retelling in small letters of the very same story which is written across the whole world in letters too large for some of us to see."

C.S. Lewis

"There is a bigger story and a better party! Living in it requires a bigger perspective and a higher capacity to have fun."

Jami and Marla

Following the process of forgiveness is the continual journey to discovering where behaviors and feelings come from. In his book *Hand-Me-Down-Genes and Second-Hand Emotions,* Steve Arterburn shows the anger of rejection as it was passed down from generation to generation. Because we all experience rejection from our parents, we have perceived the pain of rejection from our Higher Power, but we especially feel this rejection deeply from ourselves. We believe that we are not worthy of love. These feelings were then passed down to our children and they end up hurting others as well as themselves.[1]

Because of the power of love, the dark secrets that have been hidden from sight because of shame will eventually be uncovered, whether it is in the current generation or in the following generation. We are all inundated with generational junk. We are struggling with things that have not been resolved in previous generations. But the problem we run into is that some of us have to experience terrible pain before we are willing to make changes in our behavior.

Again our desire for love and intimacy shows us the way to a higher power. Take the example of a young man who was a serious partier and consistently took Ecstasy. One evening he took too much and still experiences the negative side affects. This experience finally scared him into changing his behavior for good because he realized that he could have been permanently brain damaged, or much worse. Interestingly, his father suffers from issues related to addictions. The sins of the fathers are passed down from generation to generation until one person decides to stop the cycle.[2] Fortunately for us, Jami and I chose to stop the devastating behaviors that had been passed on to us before they destroyed our lives and the lives of our children.

Life is about Relationships—it is why we are here!

Happily, your intuition installed within you creates the desire to connect intimately with those around you. Because of this, you are able to reach beyond the pain, get out of denial and have restoration in your life. Unless you are willing to begin to love yourself, loves others, forgive others and get through the pain of your past, you will not have intimacy with the special people in your life or with the Higher Power. It is only through connecting with true love that you will be able to connect with anyone else in your life. And you can only connect with love right here, right now in the present.

Fortunately love desires that you and I find the filler and lover of your soul, and then desires that you take that love given you and give it to all you come in contact. It is only through this relationship with love that you will truly have that fresh start in life, and it is our goal to reach everyone with this message who is willing to listen. One important discovery we have made is that when people share their healing story it is much more effective than if they do not share their story. It is so important that you learn to feel, and share your feelings so that your story can be transformed, and in turn the stories of others can be changed for the positive. Come join us in a bigger story, and a much better party, where you feel loved and accepted—guaranteed.

---

[1] Page 25 of *Hand Me Down Genes and Second Hand Emotions.*
[2] *Family Secrets*, Bradshaw, pp. xiii.

FOUR

Expressing Feelings

"But we need to be very careful about our tempers,
seeing all the hard times we shall have to go through
together. Won't do to quarrel, you know. At any rate,
don't begin it too soon. I know these expeditions
usually end that way: knifing one another."

C.S. Lewis, *The Silver Chair*

"We say use the key to his heart, not the
tempting dagger! It makes all the difference."

Jami and Marla

Belief vs. Feelings

Each of us has deeply held beliefs about life. I am a great "judge" of
someone else's motives and behaviors, especially Jami's. Something
to be very aware of is the difference between belief and feelings. An
easy way of identifying when a belief is coming out is when you
start to say, "I feel that . . . ." Be very careful. You may be about
to express what you think or believe *not* what you feel. So many
times in coaching we will ask how the person is feeling about the
letter they just read, and they will immediately say, "I feel that my
mother was a good person." And then a long explanation ensues.

We often stop people before they get into the story too far and
remind them that, as much as we love them and appreciate their
stories, they are not expressing their feelings. We then refer back

to the *Feeling Wheel* on page 15 and ask them to identify which feelings they are experiencing at that moment. And with some people, we have to do this over and over again because they have stuffed their feelings so far below the surface that they have great difficulty accessing them.

A good visual of this is an iceberg that only shows 10% of its size above the water, with the remaining 90% below the surface. You will remember it was not the ice above the surface that sunk the Titanic, but the ice below that wreaked havoc on the bulkhead. Telling the story is simply accessing the top 10% without getting below the surface and figuring out the real stuff our stories are made out of. If you don't access what's below the surface, you will be sunk by it and lead a life of superficiality and unrealized resolution and freedom.

PAY ATTENTION!

BE AWARE OF YOUR CORE MOTIVATIONS THAT DWELL UNDER THE SURFACE.

In the past, one of the most difficult things for me (Marla) was to express my feelings as opposed to telling the story and pointing out the negative behaviors in Jami. While the story of how the feelings came about has importance, it is far more effective to express the feelings that are related to the event. Here are some examples:

- "When we were going to be late for the party and you said that I didn't seem to care about being on time, I felt diminished, attacked and hurt."

- "When my boss told me that I was not a graceful person, I felt judged, angry and attacked."

- "When my friend asked me what in the world I do with my day, I felt misunderstood, disrespected and sad."

- "When I heard that Kayla had totaled the car, I felt fearful about her safety, frustrated and angry at her carelessness."

So many times when we are trying to get something important across to another person, we focus so much on the story that we create more frustration and confusion. And then we don't get the reaction we desire and possibly even keep getting louder and louder because we are not feeling heard. When we are able to express our feelings instead of the long story, we end up being understood and heard.

Dirty Fighting Techniques

Most of our learning about conflict resolution comes from our parents. Maybe you were like Jami and saw many fights between your parents that were highly volatile and frightening at times. Or like me who saw my parents have "loud discussions" that usually ended with my father getting what he wanted. At least that was my perception.

Other people we have coached have said that they never even saw their parents fight with each other. Actually, none of these ways of expressing are healthy. And you might think that your parents' not fighting in front of you was better, but that assumption would be wrong. Dead wrong.

When you do not see your parents fight *and in turn see them find resolution* you have no clue how to fight. Oftentimes, a person who has never seen their parents fight and a person whose parents fought very dirty get together and, boy, does the fur start to fly. Here are some of our favorite dirty fighting techniques, and some suggestions about how to fight fair:

- **Expressing "you" statements.** "You make me so angry." When you address a frustration with "I" statements and then talk about your specific feelings, you end up having a more productive conversation that probably won't meltdown into a knock-down-drag-out. So try saying, "I feel exasperated when you leave your dirty socks in the middle of the floor" instead of "You are so exasperating!"

- **Using *always* and *never*** which overstate and exaggerate the situation. "I am always the one who has to take care of the kids! You never help me." Be very aware when you use these two words. In almost every situation, when one of these two words is used, the feelings underlying the statement are feelings you have felt before that have nothing to do with your significant other. They come from somewhere very young. Take a moment to assess times when you use these words and identify the first time you felt that feeling. Journal this out so that you have more clarity, and then write a forgiveness letter regarding the event. You will find that this keeps you from going to that place when things get heated again.

- **Escalating from the issue to attacking your partner's personality**, and then to asking whether or not a relationship with this person is worth it, and verbalizing the possibility of divorce or break-up. When you love someone your intention is not to hurt them. But when things get heated, the easiest thing to want to do is lash out and be mean. Stop. Look. Listen. Take ten seconds before speaking so that you won't end up saying something you will regret later.

- **Coming at your partner at a time when they are unable to take the time to work on the problem appropriately**, like right when they are walking out the door, immediately before guests arrive, or promptly before driving into the parking lot at church. Make sure that you are bringing up important conversations at a time that will allow for the discussion to be thorough and not volatile.

- **Crucializing** – Saying something like, "If you really loved me, you would do this to make me happy." Or, "This just proves that you never loved me." Be careful about rash statements, or guilt-inducing statements. These will only create more pain. Instead, take time to think about why you are in love with your partner. Again, ten seconds can really help here. Even a time-out would be appropriate, but make sure it isn't more than 30 minutes and that you state you are not abandoning your partner but are taking a breather from the conflict.

- **Bombarding** your partner with everything that they have ever done in the past and then exclaiming that they will never change because of this "proof" that you have just expressed. Remember Rafiki in *The Lion King* when he hits Simba upside the head with his staff and an incensed Simba says, "Hey! What was that for?" Rafiki replies, "It doesn't matter. It's in the past." You need to forgive the things of the past (write your forgiveness letters as recommended in the next section) and let them stay there. It's not fair to bring things up that have been forgiven. You are allowed to call a "foul" when this happens during a fight.

- **Telling your spouse that they must be right and that there really isn't any hope for you.** This throws them completely off guard and makes you into the poor martyr. And it's just manipulative and passive-aggressive because you know you don't really mean it. You just want them to feel sorry for you and back-off. Instead of playing the martyr, swallow your pride and express your feelings without manipulation or control.

- **Twisting the blame around**. As soon as they address an issue with you, you come right back at them with an issue of your own about them. "I didn't call the insurance company, but you didn't pick up your socks that you stepped right over on your way to the shower." Now this is just childish. A tit-for-tat is not going to create a healthy dynamic. Take responsibility for your own behaviors. Buck it up, and move on. You know when you have made a mistake, so own it and forgive yourself. And forgive your spouse for bringing up your shortfall. The more you respond appropriately when conflict arises, the fewer the conflicts come up, and they will be further apart.

- **Never taking responsibility for your actions**, such as using excuses like "I forgot" or "I didn't hear you say that" or whatever else allows you to avoid responsibility and might even stop the conversation right there. Again, grow up and take responsibility for your own actions.

- **Trying to find the "solution" and not listening**. Many men will move the conversation immediately to making things work through some type of solution instead of simply listening and allowing their partners to express themselves. The first rule of thumb is to listen to your partner and their frustrations. An appropriate question to ask would be, "What do you need from me?" This helps your spouse clarify what it is that they might need, but also allows them to thank you for listening because that allowed them the time and space to figure it out on their own. Or they simply feel better because they got it off of their chest.

- And last, but not least, **abandoning your spouse by physically leaving the room or by "checking**

out" emotionally. This will cause the person being abandoned to try harder to control you through raising their voice higher, or using any number of the above techniques. Again, if you feel the desire to abandon because things have gotten out of hand, ask for a time-out and let your partner know that you need 15-30 minutes to process and then come back to the conversation, and tell them clearly that you are not abandoning them, you simply need some time to cool-off and process quietly.

It is probably pretty clear to you which of these techniques you have perfected. Take some time to process them with your partner at a time when you are both in a good space emotionally. Avoid pointing out which ones they do since this is about you and transforming your story, not about helping your significant other see their deficiencies.

FIVE

Checking In for Intimacy

"Your heart is my piñata."

Chuck Palahniuk

"No more using the bat; it is time to use a tool called 'Check-In'."

Jami and Marla

Check-in is the Key to your lover's heart. Learn this and the world will open up for you and life will take on new meaning and power. The most important thing to remember about expressing feelings is to use the "I Message" which goes like this:

1. **When** – Describe the person's behavior you are reacting to in a non-blaming and non-judgmental manner. This can also be a positive thing that you are appreciating your spouse for. It's not always negative.

2. **The effects are** – Describe the obvious or tangible effects of that behavior because your partner will benefit from knowing what your reaction to the behavior was. This will allow them to understand you more fully.

3. **I feel** – Express specific feeling from the *Feeling Wheel*. Remember, this is more important than

the story. This also allows your partner to see that you are taking responsibility for your own feelings.

4. **I'd prefer *OR* my boundary is *OR* I appreciate you for** – Let your partner know what you would prefer to happen. Be careful about boundaries because when you state one you need to be certain that you will keep it, otherwise it will not be effective.

Be careful to not discount someone else's feelings. Their feelings are real for them. Their perceptions are their reality. And it's okay because you are not responsible for their feelings, but you do love the other person and desire to understand and have empathy for their feelings.

Feeling Check and Management

Right now think of three feelings you may be experiencing. Can you do it? "Good", "Fine", "Okay", and "Alright" do not count as feelings. It is so important, as you learned from the story of Marvin and Eve you just read, to discover what you are feeling and how to express those feelings appropriately. Again—and we know we are starting to sound like a broken record here—check out the *Feeling Wheel* conveniently located on the following page to help you figure out what feelings you may be experiencing:

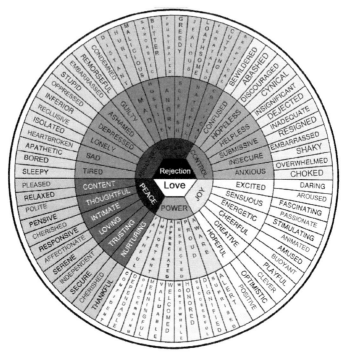

Feeling Wheel

A good technique to understanding your feelings better is to take time throughout your day to check-in with yourself about how you are feeling at that moment. Decide to set your alarm three times a day, and maybe even have your check-in time with yourself during mealtime. Pick three feeling words from the chart and write them on your calendar or in a journal. And it's okay if you have three feelings that may seem contradictory.[1]

Another great way to discover more about your strong feelings during difficult or volatile conversations, and how you can more effectively manage your feelings is to fill out the following checklist:

Part I: Doing a Feeling Check

When you are having a strong emotional reaction to a difficult conversation do you tend to feel . . .

1. <u>*Strong*</u> or <u>*Weak*</u>?
How intense is the feeling? (0 = Least intense; 10 = Most Intense)
_____ Why do you rate it this way? _____
_____
_____

2. <u>*Angry*</u> or <u>*Caring*</u>?
How intense is the feeling? (0 = Least intense; 10 = Most Intense)
_____ Why do you rate it this way? _____
_____
_____

3. <u>*Happy*</u> or <u>*Sad*</u>?
How intense is the feeling? (0 = Least intense; 10 = Most Intense)
_____ Why do you rate it this way? _____
_____
_____

4. <u>*Safe*</u> or <u>*Threatened*</u>?
How intense is the feeling? (0 = Least Intense; 10 = Most Intense)
_____ Why do you rate it this way?
_____
_____
_____

5. <u>*Fulfilled*</u> or <u>*Frustrated*</u>?
How intense is the feeling? (0 = Least; 10 = Most Intense) _____
Why do you rate it this way? _____
_____
_____

6. **_Proud_ or _Ashamed_?**
How intense is the feeling? (0 = Least; 10 = Most Intense) _____
Why do you rate it this way? _____

_____

_____

7. **_Lonely_ or _Connected_?**
How intense is the feeling? (0 = Least intense; 10 = Most Intense)
_____ Why do you rate it this way? _____

_____

_____

Part 2: Three Strongest Feelings

What are the three strongest feelings that you tend to have when you are involved in a fight or volatile conversation (refer to the *Feeling Wheel* for the most accurate feelings)?

Feeling #1: _____
1. Why did you choose this feeling? _____

_____

_____

2. What are other people doing that is causing you to feel this way?

_____

_____

_____

3. What is going on around you that is causing you to feel this way? _____

_____

_____

4. What are you thinking that is causing you to feel this way?

_____

_____

_____

5. What are you doing that is causing you to feel that way?

_____

_____

_____

Feeling #2:_____

_____

1. Why did you choose this feeling? _____

_____

_____

2. What are other people doing that is causing you to feel this way?

_____

_____

_____

3. What is going on around you that is causing you to feel this way? _____

_____

_____

4. What are you thinking that is causing you to feel this way?

_____

_____

_____

5. What are you doing that is causing you to feel that way?

_____

_____

Feeling #3:_____

1. Why did you choose this feeling? _____

_____

_____

_____

2. What are other people doing that is causing you to feel this way?

_____

_____

_____

3. What is going on around you that is causing you to feel this way? _____

_____

_____

4. What are you thinking that is causing you to feel this way?

_____

_____

_____

5. What are you doing that is causing you to feel that way?

_____

_____

_____

Part 3: Managing Your Feelings

Keeping these three feelings in mind, read each of the following statements about your ability to manage your feelings and rate how true it is on a scale of 0 to 10. ("0" means the statement is not at all true; "10" means the statement is totally true.) Place your answer on the line in front of each statement.

__ **Skill #1:** I am able to anticipate situations that are likely to provoke strong feelings and emotions.

__ **Skill #2**: I am able to recognize when I am starting to have a strong feeling or emotion.

__ **Skill #3**: I am able to stop myself from automatically reacting to the feeling without thinking it through.

__ **Skill #4**: I am able to call a time out in emotionally charged situations before my feelings become unmanageable.

__ **Skill #5**: I am able to use an immediate relaxation technique to bring down the intensity of the feeling.

__ **Skill #6**: I am able to take a deep breath and notice what I'm feeling.

__ **Skill #7**: I am able to find words that describe what I'm feeling and use the feeling list when necessary.

__ **Skill #8**: I am able to rate the intensity of my feelings using a ten-pointscale.

__ **Skill #9**: I am able to consciously acknowledge the feeling and its intensity by saying to myself, "Right now I'm feeling _____ and it's okay to be feeling this way."

__ **Skill #10**: I am able to identify what I'm thinking that is causing me to feel this way and ask myself, "How can I change my thinking in a way that will make me feel better?"

__ **Skill #11**: I am able to identify what I'm doing that is causing me to feel this way and ask myself, "How can I change what I'm doing in a way that will make me feel better?"

__ **Skill #12**: I am able to recognize and resist urges to create problems, hurt myself, or hurt other people in an attempt to make myself feel better.

__ **Skill #13**: I am able to recognize my resistance to doing things that would help me or my situation, and force myself to do those things in spite of the resistance.

__ **Skill #14**: I am able to get outside of myself and recognize and respond to what other people are feeling.

---

[1] Refer back to Rule #3 in Chapter 2.

SECTION TWO

Offer Forgiveness

SIX

Offer Forgiveness

"Every one says forgiveness is a lovely idea,
until they have something to forgive."

C S Lewis

"Forgiveness is a choice first, then when you are free because
you made the choice to forgive you will feel it."

Jami and Marla

Phillip and Mary have been married for 11 years. It was a second marriage for both of them. Like many second timers they were so delighted that their new spouse didn't have the baggage that the first one did and they were able to see past the new spouses "flaws" for some time. But baggage has a way of finding home.

The hurts from a divorce are almost never an easy recovery and if not handled properly will hurt again. Phillip is a real go-getter, super motivated, up before dawn with his successful Law Firm, and is in senior leadership in his community groups. These are all products of his work ethic. Mary prefers to stay up late, always looks fantastic, has excellent hostess skills, is socially connected, and enjoys travel. And there last name is "Perfection".

They both "knew" the honeymoon would not last and that marriage did not mean an "intimate relationship", until recently.

The dirty fighting started around the time they were planning on building their dream houseboat. This has been consistent in our observations about most people dealing with near retirement dream projects. Whether it is a boat, house, travel or just getting the "dream" car, the event is less than the expectation. Past disappointments crowd the heart and it becomes difficult to overlook the flaws in our spouse that we have ignored, agreed to step over, or just plain were not really aware of until these **disappointments started to pile up**.

So the conflict grew. First it was regarding the size and color of the boat, then between having Phillip's houseboat design built and buying an existing houseboat. The fight for control became overwhelming, and those old hurts became exposed, raw and so enflamed that even being in the same room became difficult. Fun little practical jokes became mean, hostile and vengeful. The key to the others heart long forgotten, it was now about sharpening the dagger! Before a second divorce was unthinkable, but now it seemed the only safe option.

Women being more intuitive often are first to seek help. Men would do better to listen to this more often. Men tend to think that they can boot-strap their way through anything, and especially something as personal as a relationship. The fear of losing control is often the core of resistance to getting some life coaching. When in reality, control was lost a long time ago. Men also tend to be satisfied with "status quo" and argue that their wives are too emotional or too jealous, or just plain crazy. So Mary came to see us. She of course wanted us to focus on Phillip with all his flaws and faults in this relationship. This never works.

Where to Start and Why
While it is important to know what it is you want help with, since setting goals is one of the main points of what coaching is about, a person can not make goals for another person. Developing the

foundation for meeting your own personal goals will bring you outside your control-abandonment sick-play. You can't train for a successful relationship while you're fighting a two front war, fighting off the old baggage, and the new.

We almost always ask a basic question after we can identify the core fear that a person is having now. When did you first experience this feeling in your life, as far back as you can remember? Core hurts almost always get related to parents. It is important here to say that we are not therapists and do NOT do psychotherapy. We are life coaches and address here and now concepts. We have found that forgiving our parents, as well as forgiving the deep hurts given to us by other people in our life, becomes one of the most important here-and-now issues that gets in the way of our current relationships.[1]

---

[1] NOTE: To identify your core fear, fill out the *Core Fear Identification* questionnaire developed by Gary Smalley and brought to our attention in the awesome book *The DNA of Relationships* at the end of the book under *Healing Activities*.

SEVEN

Feeling vs. Decision

"I like living. I have sometimes been wildly, despairingly, acutely miserable, racked with sorrow, but through it all I still know quite certainly that just to be alive is a grand thing."

Agatha Christie

"If we choose to live more intimately, we automatically begin living a bigger story and a better party."

Jami and Marla

So how do you learn to feel?

For me (Jami) I can only tell you how I learned to feel, and what others have learned from my experience. I grew up in a middle class home in Southern California. I remember my Dads' anger as being totally overwhelming and unreasonable. When I was seven years old, he forgot where he left his watch and spent an hour yelling and threatening me about why he could not find it. It was then that I decided that he was crazy. But that did not change the effect of his incredible rage and hurtful words had on my ability to feel.

The message I got was: my feelings were unimportant and that I had to be totally on guard for his sudden and unexplainable **RAGE**. This put me into special education from second to fifth grade, struggling to learn math and reading. So I could not tell you a feeling other than if I felt safe or not.

But the hurt was overwhelming. So I started to use alcohol and drugs at twelve years old. I used them routinely until I was nearly twenty, but then I found the love of my life. She would not tolerate any drug use, so I quit. But the drive to kill the pain took a different addiction. High risk behavior took the place of drugs and alcohol. But the ante went from dropping myself and my mountain bike off sixty foot cliffs, to serious white water rafting, to short term (unsafe) sexual encounters. Knowing that I did not want to continue this behavior but not knowing how to stop, I told Marla. While that night remains one of the most painful in each of our memories, it also was the doorway to a new more alive existence than either one of us could possibly have expected.

I entered a process where I met with a Psychiatrist who, when I told him the story you just read, asked me one question. "Where did you just go?" The question blew me away. I was a little afraid that he was crazier than me (probably what you are thinking of me right now). But what I learned was that I was really good at dissociation. Dissociation is a fancy word for *"checking out"*. I was so good at it that *I* didn't even know I was doing it. It probably saved my life. I was already suicidal enough, at least passively, thinking that if only I could have the nerve to just drive my car off the cliff, or at least swerve in front of a truck while driving 75 miles per hour.

Old skills can be a problem if we apply them past the time of their effectiveness. This *checking out* skill worked great when your three year old girl's face gets bit by the neighbor's dog, and you can hold her, speaking reassuringly while driving 80 mph. Then hold her through the painful process of stitching her face back together. But it did not serve me well when propositioned by a co-worker.

Being checked out meant that I could react like a 12 year old, just as easily as the professional I was trained to be.

Becoming aware of this skill of checking out changed everything. The next day I thought I was going to throw-up because I could feel all these emotions in my stomach. I was feeling fear, anger, joy, hurt, happiness, confusion and many more all at the same time. I never new that feelings could run so deep, and organizing how I felt was very difficult. But what a fantastic feeling, the feeling of being alive!

To recognize feelings, I had to practice expressing them. Naming each feeling was like moving from chocolate and vanilla to thirty-one flavors. Sometimes feelings have nuts in them, and sometimes nuts have feelings. :) The trick for me was to keep trying to describe what I felt to other people so that they could tell me they understood.

So I had to get with a list of feelings and practice applying feelings to events in my life. If you don't feel, you are numb. It was far easier to be numb, but worth it to do the extra work to be fully alive. Refer back to the *Feeling Wheel* on page 15 and do a "feeling check" right now. Below you will see the center of the *Feeling Wheel* that can give you a better visual of what our CORE FEELINGS are so you can move from being numb to being present:

Now back to Mary and Phillip. We discovered together that Mary's core hurt was abandonment. She felt that Phillip was abandoning her by not keeping a promise about the houseboat that he had made to her when they first got married. Answering the question about when she first felt this, she was able to identify when her ex-husband had left her. When we delved further in to the feeling she discovered that her parent's divorce and her father moving out held with them "the most hurtful feeling" of abandonment she had ever experienced. We worked through forgiving her father (See Chapter 9) and came to forgiving her ex-husband. Mary became indignant and nearly left the room, rejecting any further help from us because she felt her ex-husband did not deserve her forgiveness.

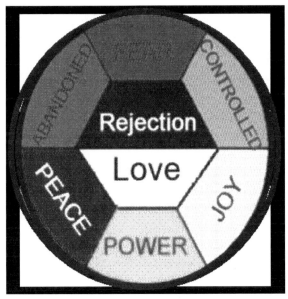

Center of Feeling Wheel

Mary's feeling of not wanting to forgive is common. Our society has made forgiveness into something it is not. Forgiveness does not excuse behavior; it does not let anyone off the "hook" or give permission for someone to hurt us or someone else again. Forgiveness is for the hurt person. It allows us to cut loose the excess baggage as well as the vain attempts at controlling the offender by withholding forgiveness. **And like all feelings it is a choice before it is a feeling.**

How do we "choose" what we feel? Feelings by nature are reactions. The meaning we give to events determines how we feel about them. **So by making good decisions about what the events of**

our lives mean, we decide how to feel. We are given training and instruction on social norms, bias, and status, but ultimately we make our own choices on these things, often rejecting the values of our parents.

This process can be done backwards or forwards. We can make better decisions about what we believe and choose to forgive. Or forgive the past decisions we have made and start making better ones now. We are aware that chemical imbalances and long term depression and anxiety particularly can require a psychiatrist's help but we always hope for a short term medical intervention relying on the discipline of taking every thought captive and not riding thoughts and feelings like a train.

So *we* decide the meaning of the events, and thus how we feel about them. When Mary was hurt by her father leaving it was because she assigned the blame on herself. Taking things personally is one of the great mistakes we make as humans. A wise friend once told us, "don't worry what other's think of you because they rarely do". Generally people are so wrapped up in their lives that they are too preoccupied to think, criticize, or evaluate you and your life. Yet we choose to worry about what people think, and take things personally because of our own narcissism.

EIGHT

Memory and Neuro-Pathways

"There are only two ways to live your life. One is as though nothing is a miracle. The other is as though everything is a miracle."

Albert Einstein

"Old habits in our thinking are changed only with a daily discipline to spot the old skills and speak change in the language of our mind."

Jami and Marla

It is important at this point to understand memory and how it affects our belief about ourselves. As we mentioned earlier, our brains start recording memory at the beginning of the third trimester. So for three months before we are born we are taking notice. But not just any notice. Memory is essentially a function of connecting neurons, and neurons connected with strong emotional tags stick together more powerfully. To make this more understandable, check out the following quote from Dr. Thomas Verney's book, *The Secret Life of the Unborn Child: How You Can Prepare Your Unborn Baby for a Happy, Healthy Life,*

"What could produce the roots of a deep-seated, long-term anxiety in an unborn child? One possibility is his mother's smoking. In a remarkable study done several years ago, Dr. Michael Lieberman showed that an unborn child grows emotionally agitated (as measured by the quickening of his heartbeat) each time his mothers thinks of having a cigarette. She doesn't even have to put it to her lips or light a match; just her *idea* of having a cigarette is enough to upset him. Naturally, the fetus has no way of knowing this mother is smoking—or thinking about it—but he is intellectually sophisticated enough to associate the experience of her smoking with the unpleasant sensation it produces in him. This is caused by the drop in his oxygen supply . . ."

Think of your earliest memories, and they often have a strong emotional tag. This becomes a function of the amygdala – a tiny, almond-shaped memory regulator in your mid-brain. The amygdala has the ability to scan your conscious and unconscious thoughts hundreds of times a second, taking every bit of sensory information you are receiving and checking it against your existing memory. So when you are "tagged" with a familiar piece of information that is potentially dangerous, your amygdala sets you up to fight or to run away or sometimes moves you to participate in some type of stress-avoidance behavior. If we don't take charge of this process—this is the "sick-play" we talked about earlier when the amygdala only has negative tools to use—it can cripple us from growing beyond what worked for us when we were twelve.[1]

Tickets for the Subway

Another way this works against us is anxiety. The best glue for neurons is probably fear, but anxiety is a close relative. So for Mary it would look like this: having had an uncomfortable fight with Phillip, she would go to bed at night and think, "Oh no, it's happening again." Then her mind would immediately go to the core hurt of "I will always be alone" (loneliness and rejection being the Core Fears).

This is called the *worry-fear cycle*. Her mind would process this over and over again which would cause her to worry more which would then cause her to have more fear and would end up with her becoming exhausted from losing sleep. And because of her loss of sleep, she was unable to think clearly and became angrier until she came to the point of completely ignoring Phillip for days at a time until he "agreed" with her about how insensitive he had been toward her feelings and asked her forgiveness. This acquiescence sadly allowed Mary to avoid any responsibility for her actions and behaviors and kept her stuck in bitterness and resentment.

Something important to take note of here is that every period of exhaustion leads to a period of depression. Good sleep is very important for recovery, whether the recovery is of an emotional or a physical nature.

We call this the "ticket and the subway". The "ticket" is the uncomfortable fight Mary and Phillip had, the "turnstile" is the fear, and the "subway" is whatever negative thought you may have that makes you believe that you are not worthy of love. **Too often we ride the train of the "old" feelings right into a wall**. For Mary it was the fear of being controlled and ultimately having to be alone and rejected yet again that made her want to control. Below is a word-picture that will help you understand how a foundational core fear of rejection affects us, and how a foundation of acceptance and love can stop the vicious cycle of pain and bitterness in our lives.

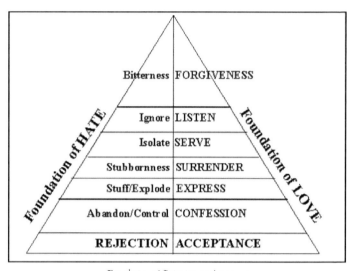

Foundation of Rejection or Acceptance

Once you're on the subway it is too late to stop the process. You have already been hijacked into negative thinking. What has to happen is for you to get better at recognizing this negative neural pathway and consciously change the process earlier and earlier. We like to use the words "Cancel, Cancel". Saying them out loud breaks the cycle, gets you out of the turnstile and allows you a moment to replace the picture of doom that you are replicating with your intended outcome. It is important that you have a clear picture of what you desire your life to be—the whole purpose of coaching is to get closer and closer to the healed and whole picture you have created for yourself—or you will not get anywhere.

Make your picture complete with the location, people, objects and values you want to see in your life. Make it clear and IMAX large. After you have shrunk the old self-destructive images and have made them dark and put it behind the moon, it is time to focus on your goal picture. We know a guy who uses this technique and charges by the cure, and he is very rich. Also you can use what the famous sleep doctor, who also happened to be an atheist at the

time, Dr. Borkevek recommends to his sleep disturbed patients —
Christian prayer.

---

[1] *Emotional Intelligence* written by Daniel Goleman is incredible, and has a plethora of information regarding this emotional takeover of the brain.

NINE

Focused Journaling

"Wouldn't you like to meet every encounter with a fresh burst of wisdom? This is exactly what happens when we take time to consult [the Higher Power] on a daily basis."

Rhonda Wilson

"We began experiencing LOVE personally and deeply for the first time because of this powerful style of journaling."

Marla and Jami

(Marla) It was 1992 when my relationship with my Higher Power was truly transformed. I had been a believer in the Higher Power all my life, but had never really experienced Love on an intimate level. There were moments during mountaintop-type experiences, but not deeply and consistently. Then Jami and I attended a powerful journaling seminar.[1] The stories I heard about the results of asking specifically for what one wanted were unbelievable, and the presenter's life and experience with love seemed so alive. When I arrived back home I made a commitment to get up early every morning before our daughters got up (Kayla was two and Ariel was one) to try out this new way of experiencing deeper, more intimate love. It was unbelievable what began to happen in my heart. I was transformed from a volunteer-junky-because-it-was-my-duty into someone who wanted to do whatever I could for my Higher Power because love was truly living inside of me.

To this point I (Marla) was completely lost, did not know who I was outside of being a wife and mother. I had no idea what I wanted for myself or that I even could want something for myself! This style of journaling brought me to knowing what I wanted – greater intimacy for myself and for those couples we work with. We explain this more in our book *Our Real Journey*.

Jami even wrote down forty of the most outlandish requests and within two years they had all been clearly answered. Not always the answers Jami would have liked, but looking back he knows that love took over and did it's thing. Go figure! The one thing that was clear to us was that journaling is a very powerful, healing tool; and it is transformational. Little did we know that our lives would be changed exponentially. It has been the best of times; it has been the worst of times. But it has all been worth it. **I would do it all over again – including going through the most painful time of my life** – to be where I am with Jami, and to be where I am in my relationship with the Higher Power.

The Power of Prayer

As we mentioned before, every memory from the last three months in the womb to the present moment are stored in your subconscious brain and are continually accessed to determine your current behavior. While my mom was in her third trimester of an unexpected pregnancy with me, she was struggling with the idea of having three children. She was tired, frustrated and overwhelmed by the thought of having another baby now that her two children were six and four years old.

Apparently, I took this to heart and when I was born I was "an angel baby", as my mother would always say. I would wake up smiling and caused little trouble. I was making sure not to put more pressure on my mother. As I grew up I unconsciously took this false belief on as my goal in life—don't rock the boat, make everyone happy and take care of everybody else before myself. This worked well for everybody else, but I completely lost my identity. I was a true codependent—a dysfunction that is associated with or results from focusing on the needs and behavior of others. Now, I am a recovering codependent, discovering what I like and who I really am outside of pleasing others. Journaling allowed me to confront the false belief that my job in life was to take care of everyone else, ignoring my needs, and to replace it with the worthiness of love that I feel now that can only come from the only source of Love.

It is important to utilize the power of love so that you are able to confront each false belief given to you from your childhood and replace it with a specific truth from powerful intuition. Love's desire for you is to replace the negative thought processes that keep you trapped in uncertainty and confusion with reality — truth and love!

Science has proven time and again the benefits of meditating on truth. From physical to emotional healing, to the healing of the soul, those who have the hope and strength of meditation with gratefulness are more likely to have true healing, peace and joy. This style of journaling moves your unconscious thoughts from passively dictating your behavior to being an active agent in attaining your goals and living an authentic, whole life. By giving your will to your Higher Power and accepting healing for your soul you align yourself with love and intuition, your counselor in this journey of your soul to the truth, light and peace that passes all understanding.

The Process of Journaling
One thing to note is that before I begin journaling, I read a chapter from an inspirational, truth-telling book I am currently experiencing. Then, the bottom line for journaling is to come to experience love through *magnifying* beauty, intuition, strength and integrity in my life; *confiding* in Love and grace your inconsistencies

and unrealities; *surrendering* your requests, *affirming* love in your life through gratitude, and *attending* to what love is speaking to your heart. Love will give you joy and true peace. You will be free from the bondage of pain and this will make you whole! I know because I see this happen in my life daily as the layers of the onion peel away one by one, and I am released to receive. Visualize putting all your burdens, pain, sorrow, and rejection in your hands, holding them out, and releasing them. This leaves your hands completely open to receive beauty, intuition, strength and integrity.

Magnify – To glorify, praise, extol.
The first step in journaling is magnifying and praising those things that are beautiful, full of grace, and peaceful in your life. By acclaiming Love as the creator of all life and beauty you are acknowledging and receiving grace. Once you recognize that Love is in control you are able to find powerful security. Beginning your meditation time by magnifying the amazing power of love in your life, your mind can focus completely on it and it's great power!

Love deserves our adoration, and what better way to adore our Higher Power than to list the powerful, beautiful characteristics of such love? Pick a poem of praise and gratefulness and write it out in your own words, or list alphabetically the characteristics you adore about Love. Magnifying your spiritual connection to Love sets the tone for your entire meditation time. It focuses your attention on love and humility, not on your selfishness and pain.

Quote Your Favorite Authors:
"...Love is not love
Which alters when it alteration finds,
Or Bends with the remover to remove.
O, no! It is an ever-fixed mark,
That looks on tempests and is never shaken.
It is the star to every wandering bark,
whose worth's unknown, although his height be taken.

-- William Shakespeare

<u>Personalize Poems:</u>

> "True beauty is in the way I laugh, True beauty is in my eyes, True beauty is how I act, True beauty is inside . . . True beauty within me, True beauty is always there, True Beauty can't be covered with makeup, True beauty means true love, True beauty can't be baked up, True beauty is the flight of a dove, True beauty has no flaws For True beauty is all that matters after all."
> -- Jean Pullman

<u>Sing a Favorite Song About Beauty:</u> Sing your favorite song or write it out in your journal and meditate on the words. It's also very powerful to listen to your favorite uplifting music while you journal.

Focus your adoration on Love's character and not on the gifts given to you (this will be accomplished in the *Affirmatin* section). Magnifying your Higher Power is about expressing the glorious love you feel all around you!

Confide – To tell or talk about as a secret; to entrust.
In confiding in your journal your negative, unhealthy and unreal behaviors there is great strength. This strength comes if you are able to be specific and honest. It is easy to be general or vague in presenting your negative nature in your journaling, but this does not allow you to make adjustments to your behavior and work on your negative impulses. Becoming conscious of your negative behaviors allows you to be more self-expressed and gives you the grace to accept your shortcomings and do something about them. In doing this you are able to be specific and honest.

There is no fear in being real in this time with your Higher Power. You are already known completely and intimately by love. No other person will see your journal, and in this knowledge there is safety. Identifying your unloving nature and admitting it openly in this journaling time is extremely effective in beginning the process of forgiving yourself. Your life will become radically different as Love brings you from humble confessor to the powerful wielder of forgiveness.

There was once a man who claimed that he had not done anything contrary to love in seven years. Was he proud of this claim? Absolutely. Was he being realistic? Probably not. Certainly he wasn't able to step outside of his self-serving, prideful behavior. The very act of bragging shows a lot about what's going on internally. But many people fall into similar traps. By failing to take a fearless moral inventory you hold on to your unloving nature and do yourself a terrible injustice. Thus, every time you are critical, gossip, tell a "white lie," raise your voice in anger and essentially fail to love your neighbor as yourself you have the opportunity to confide this in Love and be healed.

Surrender: To give up to another's power or control.
After acknowledging true beauty and love and then admitting your need for deeper Love in your life you are ready to surrender your requests and desires. Once again, you are aligning your desires with love because you are willing to release to receive.

There is nothing Love cannot accomplish in your life. It is only by listing specific requests that your mind consciously and unconsciously can work towards attaining these goals. Many times one asks for things that they are not ready to receive or they ask for things contrary to what would be loving and good in their life. By journaling your specific requests you are able to track answers to your requests and also your own spiritual growth.

As you grow, you mature and become attune to deeper Love and intuition in your life.

General Request List: Break up your request into whatever categories fit your needs such as family, personal, work, friends, etc. These requests may take years to be fulfilled but do not be discouraged. Jami meditated daily on his desire to have healing in himself, and that this healing would result in a truly intimate relationship with me, and it finally happened! What an incredible result from this time focusing on Love!

Daily Request List: As part of your daily writing, allow for new requests that may not need to be on your General Request List. An example of this would be journaling the desire for a meeting to go well that day, or meditating on the strength of Love to make it through a rough family situation.

Affirm: **to say positively, declare firmly, assert to be true, to make valid.**
Here you make use of a powerful tool of the mind. By having a thankful heart, you further validate Love and power in your life. Furthermore, you record new and powerful beliefs into your subconscious mind that allow you to react out of the power-base of love rather than react from old habits.

Your amazing worthiness comes from Love — know it, feel it and completely accept it! Each day write out the following affirmation and fill in the blank with what you need to experience from your Higher Power: "Thank you for the healing of my mind because I am worthy of _____." This affirmation written over and over again, day by day, will gel in your mind and become reality. The reason for this is because it is absolutely true. You are worthy of true intimacy, love, grace, power, intuition, beauty, strength and integrity.

Affirmations are wonderful healers of any hurt and can take away any loss and fill it with Love. Deep inside of us we all have a Love-shaped hole. Even though you may be trying to fill that hole with anything but Love, the emptiness you feel at the core of your being will not go away until you allow Love to pour into you and make you completely whole.

<u>Affirmation Examples</u>: *I am grateful for my good health. Thank you for Love revealed to me today. I am grateful for the knowledge that I am powerless without Love. I am grateful for my family. I am grateful for peace, joy and love in my life today.*

Affirmations are for the past, present and future because you know that Love has taken over and will empower you to be full of grace. It's awesome to look back in your journal and see where there are specifically answered requests, and to thank your Higher Power in this section of your journaling time.

<u>Attend:</u> To pay attention, give heed, to devote or apply oneself, to be in readiness.
Here you simply listen in your quiet place. Once you have taken the previous steps of Magnifying, Confiding, Surrendering and Affirming your mind will be clear from the clatter of life. In this quiet place alone you can hear the still, small voice of Love.

When you hear the voice of Love, write down the impressions you receive so that they are recorded and you can take action upon them and not forget them. Listen carefully. It is a rare person who says, "It will be my pleasure to take a few men and storm the fortified city" or "Yes, I will allow Love to flow through me no matter what comes against me today." Listening is a lost art. You would do well to capture this skill and then, with a glad heart, share what you have heard.

Focused Journaling as a Stress Reliever

There have been many studies that show focused journaling actually reduces stress. Interestingly, a study from the University of Florida and Wayne State University "shows most older adults use prayer more than any other alternative health remedy to help manage the stress in their lives. In addition, nurse researchers found that prayer is the most frequently reported alternative treatment used by seniors to feel better or maintain health in general."[1]

Focused Journaling as a Life Saver

So many my journaled requests have been answered in miraculous ways, and I have been given me such hope and comfort through my experience with Love. Ten years ago, when my life seemed to be completely unraveling, it came down to just my Higher Power and I. But every morning I was given me what I needed to get through that day. The very morning I was crying out in desperation, expressing how angry I was at Jami for betraying me, and then expressing how I didn't know if I should forgive Jami and have restoration in our relationship, my very next reading said this:

> "Therefore each of you must put off falsehood and speak truthfully to his neighbor, for we are all members of one body. *'In your anger do not sin':* **Do not let the sun go down while you are still angry, and do not give the devil a foothold**. He who has been stealing must steal no longer, but must work, doing something useful with his own hands, that he may have something to share with those in need. Do not let any unwholesome talk come out of your mouths, but only what is helpful for building others up according to their needs, that it may benefit those who listen. . .*Get rid of all bitterness, rage and anger, brawling and slander, along*

> **with every form of malice. Be kind and compassionate**
> **to one another, forgiving each other. . ."**

Wow! Love spoke directly to my anger and my unforgiveness, and assured me that not only was I to forgive Jami, but that Love was healing Jami and that I needed to throw away my bitterness and allow Jami back into my heart. My Higher Power offered me this safe place so that I could trust again. What an incredible miracle!

We realize that journaling can be difficult for some personalities, but we have never seen anyone who has journaled for at least 6 weeks not receive significant blessings.

---

[1] Becky Tirabassi's seminar on journaling in 1992 was phenomenal, and we are certain she is still as incredible today.

[2] *Seniors Use Prayer To Cope With Stress; Prayer No. 1 Alternative Remedy,* ScienceDaily [*Jan. 5, 2001*] http://www.sciencedaily.com/releases/2001/01/010103113921.htm

TEN

Letter writing

*"To send a letter is a good way to go somewhere
without moving anything but your heart."*

Phyllis Theroux

*"You haven't forgiven until you have written
it down and read it out loud!"*

Marla and Jami

Often people tell us that they have "forgiven all that." Rarely is
this the case. So, here is how you know if you have forgiven:

- First, you have told them in person that you
  have forgiven them.

- Second, you have allowed for them to make
  amends (they may not make amends, or admit
  their wrongdoing, but you have given them the
  opportunity to do so).

- Third, when you think about this person, or the
  circumstances surrounding your hurt, you don't
  still feel angry.

- And fourth, you have asked for forgiveness for
  your part, even if the only thing you have done
  wrong is to withhold forgiveness. In preparation

for that conversation, or if it is unsafe for emotional abuse reasons or physically impossible (the person is dead or you are in the witness protection program), we recommend writing letters of forgiveness. The format is simple and is given below.

Forgiveness and Empowerment Letter

Dear_____:

What I miss about you is:

What I don't miss about you is:

When you:

I felt:

I choose to forgive you now.

I regret I never told you:

I appreciate you when:

(Close it out and sign it.)

We do not recommend sending this letter for two reasons. First, by writing these letters you are in a process that will likely change your perspective and the content will possibly change. And second, because we think it is important to burn it, or flush it. This creates a powerful visual image that releases the pain involved.

It is a simple process to follow. We recommend you use a yellow legal pad and a red felt-tip pen for the letters. Yellow and red just seem to draw attention and help glue the healing synapses together in the subconscious.[1] We ask that you write out each of the segments and complete the sentences. Even if you don't miss anything about the person just say so. It actually helps make the process clearer when you write it out. The other thing that people resist is actually writing "I chose to forgive you now." We have already discussed why this is a choice, but it is important to remember that all your feelings are a choice before they are felt.

Turn the Key for Peace

Here is the key point in what we have discovered in this process. Writing a letter back from each person you are forgiving. This is an even simpler format. Just complete the sentences with what you need to hear from each of these people. Write it as if they were whole and healthy. In other words, they are in an emotional state where they are able to tell you exactly what you need to hear without shame, malice, hurt, manipulation or guilt. We have found that writing a letter back can close the issue and keep it from returning. It is also very revealing as to what your heart needs to hear. When you put the pen to the paper and allow yourself to be creative in what you might need to hear from this person, often surprising things are revealed.

On the next page you will find the format for the letter back. Remember that you are writing yourself FROM the person whom you wrote the letter to as if they are completely healed and able to say the things you need to hear from them.

Letter Back

Dear (self):

I am sorry for (*Regret*):

I was wrong (*Responsibility*).

If I could have, I would have _____ to make it right (*Restitution*).

I will not do it again (*Repenting*).

Thank you for forgiving me (*Forgiveness*).

(Close it and sign the person's name you have forgiven.)

This is a very powerful process. It may be necessary to seek professional advice while completing these letters. We have benefited from Christian counseling and found a mentor in the psychologist who gave us the first version of the *Empowerment Letter*. Thank you, Russ![2]

List of Those to Forgive

We are not about making anyone wrong or responsible for our pain. We are about recognizing that none of us are perfect and there is pain in most relationships. Forgiveness letters will surprise you in what they reveal in you.

- Dad – We recommend that anyone writing the letters start with their father. Dads are often more concrete than Moms because our issues with them tend to be easily accessed and available to us without much digging.

- Mother is next, but here is our disclaimer: it is okay to have hurt feelings about your mother. Of course we cast no blame on anyone's parents. Parents do the best they can most of the time. We can never know the difficulties they may have overcome. This letter is for you first. Recognizing the feelings that resulted from your living with another human being are important, so move forward through this process.

- Siblings – you may not feel that all of your siblings need to be forgiven, but simply write the letters and see what happens.

- Grandparents, or other people closely connected to your family.

- Then to ex-girlfriends and boyfriends, and/or spouses. Often times the women we work with will write a letter to all the men who hurt them, and add specific names in the "when you, I felt" section.

- Institutions, past and/or present. This can be tricky but worth the extra work. We have found a significant hurt from the churches and/or work places we have been involved with. It is a shame that what could be the safest place on earth is often the most hurtful.

- God – Churches can give us a horrible picture of who God is, so if that is the case with you this letter will rid your life of that false god and allow you to begin to get acquainted with the real God who has been waiting for His letter a long, long time. But again, just follow the format. Take what works and move on.

- Yourself – Self. That person you have been needing to forgive but just have not made the time to do it. It is time. This one can feel a bit schizophrenic. But try not to out-think yourself. It is forgiving yourself that really prepares you to have the forgiveness conversations that you need to have. Symptoms of self forgiveness are: Not taking things personally, extending forgiveness to others, being present, not holding a grudge, no fear of judgment, no anxiety, and of course having a fully disclosed relationship with your spouse.

We recommend burning these letters and letters back after each category. We say a blessing of release with our friends when they have written their letters and shared them with us.

Everyone who has done this sees direct benefit, and we can feel the clarity they begin to have that day. The most common feeling following the burning of letters is "relief". And after a few days have gone by to digest that relief, people often tell us they have a sense of peace they have never felt before. Awesome!

---

[1] Think of icons such as McDonalds, Shell and the website for Invite Inc. – www.inviteinc.org.

[2] Russ is a powerfully quiet man who is very private, has more work than he ever wanted and is so humble and gracious we are not using his last name.

SECTION THREE

Vision Future Intimacy

ELEVEN

Key-Dagger

> *"Among men, sex sometimes results in intimacy; among women, intimacy sometimes results in sex."*

Barbara Cartland

> *"It's all about what happens between the ears way before it happens between the sheets!"*

Jami and Marla Keller

Vision Future Intimacy

Andria was angry. Martin had signed up for another four years of military service and she was pregnant. He had not even talked to her about it. This meant he would likely have to do another tour in Iraq. For his part, when he signed up he was told that he would not have to go back to Iraq, but things had changed. He was scheduled to deploy in six weeks. She was incensed, stressed out and not coping well. She was on the "subway", with a knife in her hand. Well, not really but it would not have taken much to get her there.

To understand why Andria was so hurt and desperate we took a step into her past with her. We discovered that Martin's apparent disregard for her needs and her feelings of being abandoned were hurting her where she had already been hurt. Before she was nine her father suddenly went from being a pillar in the community to abandoning his wife and kids for a life of drugs and women. This left Andria deeply wounded with a core hurt of abandonment and rejection right when she needed her father the most. And now it appeared that her husband was abandoning her right when she needed him the most. (We tend to hurt others where they have been hurt before first because there is still a sore spot and there is also a subconscious awareness that if we touch the sore spot we get a bigger reaction. We want to find out "how much does this person care?")

Andria chose Martin because he has the key to her heart, but he inadvertently ended up using the dagger, placing it deep into the core of her old, unresolved pain. This is a common occurrence in relationships because of our failure to recognize our core pain, and the pain of our partners, thus damaging each other further in the confusion of it all. Within each relationship the partners have matching emotional issues. Not necessarily the same circumstances, but most definitely the same core pain. **And this is how we end up making each other crazy.**

As for Martin, his core pain was a result of being controlled by his mother, as well as other authority figures. Andria was attracted to his confidence and independence that was a result of his rejection of being controlled. His initial reaction to being controlled, or simply the fear of being controlled, was to run as quickly and as far away from it as possible. As a teenager, he joined the military to escape from the control he felt at home. The irony being that when Andria confronted him about his inconsiderate choices and determined to control the situation he immediately checked out of the conversation and abandoned her emotionally, causing her to try and control the situation even more intensely. As you can see, this turned in to a vicious cycle of control-abandonment, or dagger versus dagger.

The result of understanding these concepts through coaching led Martin and Andria to communicate more effectively about their core needs and feelings, and to begin to work as a team in achieving them. The Key-Dagger is where the control-abandonment cycle, sick-play and subway meet. Our soul mate has our match in all three of these scenarios, so they hold the key to our hearts. Unfortunately, on the other side of the key is our dagger that often wreaks havoc on a relationship. Here is a graphical illustration of what we are referring to:

Rejection: Control/Abandonment

In order to understand why we fight it is very important to take into consideration that we all have been hurt. Our core hurts are rejections. A rejection is anytime we are told in any way that we are not "okay". In other words, any time anyone in our world tries to control us or leave us (abandon). We re-enter a contest with the people that are closest to us in an attempt to regain that control. In doing so, we can inadvertently lose everything we are trying to gain, and more.

Remember, there are two basic foundations in this life: Rejection and Love, as seen in the graphic in Chapter 7. If we can operate from the foundation of love, then it is possible to have peace and joy with the relationships in our lives. If we operate from rejection, we are going to find fear and anger and much unneeded drama.

In order to move from rejection to love as our foundation for living we must learn to forgive the pain we have had and learn how to express what we are feeling right now. One exercise you can bring yourself through is to ask yourself "When did I first feel this powerful Control or Abandonment?" If we can identify when a feeling first entered our life, we can work on the forgiveness process through the letter writing we described earlier in this book. Then when we feel that oh so familiar feeling the next time, we can express it healthfully. When we have the key-dagger agreement that all our feelings are real and our partner is not responsible for our feelings, and we express to them that we have a feeling of control or abandonment (or both), suddenly the feeling does not control us and leaves our body painlessly. This is a big move for most people. It requires forgiveness as well as the key-dagger agreement so that there is not a threat of your feelings creating pain for your partner.

When a partner is not willing to make this agreement it is more difficult, but the process can be done. This requires that you are very clear about your feelings. Again this is accomplished by a complete forgiveness process and practicing expressing your feelings. Then you have to make a priority list and let your partner know how you feel one issue at a time and at a pace they can handle.

You will also need the extra patience of explaining your feelings remembering that this does not require your partner to take responsibility for your feelings. They of course are responsible for their behavior, and when there is hurt they need to be present to the need for change, because the fact remains we are either growing together or apart at all times. No one stays stagnant, so if your marriage isn't getting better then it's probably getting worse. The best way we have discovered to grow together and get better is through "Check –in".

TWELVE

Check-in Again

"If you want to go quickly, go alone. If you want to go far, go together."
African proverb

"With the gift of listening comes the gift of healing."
Catherine de Hueck

"Love is touching souls."
Joni Mitchell

"Learning 'check-in' saved our marriage."
Jami and Marla

And again the answer to more intimacy and healing is checking-in. Marla and I learned how to follow through with our healing ten years ago from Recovering Couples Anonymous. There was a twelve step teaching, then the couples would separate in to small groups of no more than three couples.[1] The check-in rules are simple. Face each other with "soft eyes" and without legs or arms crossed to show that you are open. We chose to have Jami go first on odd days and Marla on even days. The other person does not speak until the first says "I Pass". This is the format to follow:

- First describe a real event like "Today, at breakfast when we talked . . ."

- Second express two or three core feelings (refer to the feeling wheel) in regards to that event. ("Today, at breakfast when we talked <u>I felt hurt, unworthy and controlled</u>.")

- The third step is optional and can be an affirmation or a boundary. ("Today, at breakfast when we talked I felt hurt, unworthy and controlled, <u>and in the future I would like time to process my feelings before we make a final decision</u>.")

We recommend that check-in is done every day for at least twenty-one days. Then do it at least twice a week without fail. We knew our relationship was going to make it when we got into a "hot conversation" and were able to follow this format instead of melting in to dirty fighting.

Something magical happens when you can speak your feelings. Somehow the control goes away when you say "I feel controlled". Anger dissolves and frustration finds a way out when you are able to communicate in this manner consistently. It is just like teaching a two-year-old to use their words instead of slamming their body on the ground and crying. Suddenly understanding is possible, empathy replaces confusion and joy becomes an option.

This of course takes practice, and it is absolutely mandatory that you follow the rules about feelings in the first chapter, as well as remember to avoid dirty fighting techniques. Fundamentally, feelings are real. It is self-destructive to deny yours, or anyone else's. The best breakthroughs are here in check-in. We have made it a habit of forming groups that can practice safely together and keep each other accountable.[2]

Taking it a step further, after the second person has gone, you can then mirror each other's feelings. This is essentially repeating the feelings you heard the other say, with empathy, so that they know you heard them completely. You then can ask them, "Is that what you wanted to convey?" Being corrected is not bad; it actually leads to better understanding. This is how Martin and Andria were able to cope with the distance while he was preparing to go to Iraq for his second tour. Being able to communicate clearly while they were apart kept their marriage together.

Here is an example of a check-in between Jami and I:

JAMI→

- "*When* you don't support me when I am disciplining the kids, *I feel* hurt, frustrated and disappointed. *In the future* I would ask that you support me while I am having a conversation with the girls and wait for later to talk about it."

- "*When* you try to control me *like* when I want to go out with the guys and you express frustration I *feel guilty*, manipulated and sad. *In the future* I would like to discuss this matter and come to a compromise."

- "*When* you are supportive when I discipline the kids *like* the other day *I feel* loved, appreciated and respected. *Thank you for supporting me.*"

- "I love you and *I pass.*"

MARLA→

- "*When* you abandon me, *like* the other day when you played your game after I went to bed, *I felt* hurt, invisible and unworthy. *In the future* I would like us to go to bed together at least four nights out of seven."

- "*When* you are unaware of my needs, *like* when you left me to do all the work in the kitchen I feel abandoned, disrespected and unimportant. *In the future* I will be more intentional about asking for help."

- "*When* you care for me *like* this morning with making me breakfast I feel loved, valued and visible. *Thank you* for caring for me."

- "I love you and with that *I'll pass*."

---

[1] NOTE: Nearly everyone could benefit from working the twelve steps. We appreciated Keith Miller's book *A Hunger for Healing*.

[2] If you are interested in Recovering Couples Anonymous, check out their website for a meeting near you (*www.recovering-couples.org*).

SECTION FOUR

Enter In To Strength and Integrity

THIRTEEN

Community Accountability

"The first duty of a human being is to assume the right functional relationship to society -- more briefly, to find your real job, and do it."

Charlotte Perkins Gilman

"Everyone's job is to build and guard healthy intimacy, it is in fact the only reason why we are here."

Marla and Jami

Community is your family and the people you choose to be family. We are finding fewer and fewer people have safe extended family near to them. When family is not a place where you feel safe, loneliness creeps in and isolation can wreak havoc on your heart. Old friends and family often have difficulty adjusting to an individual's growth.

Change is very difficult just for our thinking process, much less trying to explain to those who are used to having our old dysfunctions around to keep them company. In order to grow, everyone needs a safe place. Finding that place with people that are willing to be safe is very difficult. Most often there are failures in the places where we would expect support. Old friends, churches and families disappoint everyone at sometime, and especially when we are trying to grow and change. Most community groups lack deep connection and realness, and are not safe for true intimacy.

That is the true-but-useless part of this change story. It has to be said, but it does little good.

What to do about it? Find a safe place – a place where it is safe for you to share core feelings and be supported. We have found that twelve step groups are very effective and have the key components for growth: shared values, mentoring and a supportive environment. For relationships, Recovering Couples Anonymous is extremely helpful. RCA is not everywhere but we have known couples who have driven eight hours one way to make a group, and there are online groups as well. When your reason for getting what you need is big enough, you will find a way. But you have to be willing to make change happen.

As you make change happen, you will need someone to share with, and as a couple you will need another couple (at least) that are willing to share healthfully. Always, once you have learned that feelings are real and need sharing in order to have healthy relationships, you will have to teach others how this works. The rules are simple, and they apply in every situation. The rules are:

1. Feelings are real.

2. Feelings are the responsibility of the person feeling them.

3. When hearing someone's feelings, it is appropriate to listen and respond with "I hear that you feel these feelings and I know they are real."

Sorry to be the bearer of such news, but this is hard work and requires consistency, grace and forgiveness. Accountability is scary, but only until it becomes the tool that exposes reality in our lives. Big breakthroughs happen when you are all-in, and you dump all pretenses. This is honesty. Honesty about who we are, what our behaviors are, and how we feel sets us free from anxiety, fear and depression.

Finding people with shared values is difficult and will never be perfect. To begin, one has to know what one's values are in order to find a group with similar values. This book can not be a complete guide, but we know that at our core, our desire is to be appreciated, loved and accountable to our personal goals. One very important clue to know that you are achieving this is finding high levels of satisfaction in serving others.

The next step is to find a mentor. Almost no great person in history was without a good mentor. Again there are no perfect people, so you will not find a perfect mentor. But good people are out there and are willing to share their experience if you can find a way to spend time with them and ask for the feedback that you need.

And last, you must have a supportive environment. Almost no one can change with negative talk being spoken against them. Simply do not tolerate it around you. This is a good place to say, **"This is not okay with me!"** and move yourself away from the negative forces. More and more we are finding that community is the answer to what hurts us most. Adding your personal accountability to a small group and growing that group in depth and numbers will get you far as you seek a deeper and more satisfying experience. Ultimately this requires us to choose or grow a better community where the key ingredients are present.

FOURTEEN

Understanding Crazy Making and Healing

"No other gods, only me. No carved gods of any size, shape, or form of anything whatever, whether of things that fly or walk or swim. Don't bow down to them and don't serve them because I am God, your God, and I'm a most jealous God, punishing the children for any sins their parents pass on to them to the third, and yes, even to the fourth generation of those who hate me. But I'm unswervingly loyal to the thousands (generation) who love me and keep my commandments."

The Second Commandment –
Exodus 20:3-5 from the Message Bible

"As we become the person we were created to be, the old family issues impact us less and less, be become an agent of healing."

Marla and Jami

In one of our weekend seminars in Phoenix, Arizona came a beautiful couple, both gorgeous and in their early twenties, him tall muscular with leadership personality, her tan and fit just off the gym floor. They had been married just less than three months, after more than a year engagement. Very much in love but sensing something, Janelle worked very hard to get Justin to our seminar. After the first session's break, he came back and announced to the twenty-plus people that he was already in danger of cheating on his beautiful bride, but was committed to using the tools we were offering to keep this from happening.

This was rigorous honesty. Justin was brave enough to share this insight because Janelle was brave enough to hear it. This is not unusual behavior, and extramarital affairs are common for men, and rising fast for young women. What made Justin's revelation so brave was that it was breaking a pattern of family secrets that was very strong, and destructive. His mother's affair and his uncle's murder were two strongly kept secrets that were creating dynamic barriers in this new marriage that may not have been acted on right away but would have cracked the foundation that would certainly falter later.

Family secrets is the topic of entire books, two of the best being *Family Secrets* by John Bradshaw and *Secrets of Your Family Tree* by Dave Carder, M.A., Dr. Earl Henslin, Dr. John Townsend, Dr. Henry Cloud and Alice Brawand, M.A. Both are books that transformed our lives and helped us see through some of the traps that were laid before us, sometimes before we were even born. It is painful to see alcoholism, sexual abuse, and other hurtful issues passed down in a family.

Justin's pattern of hiding his mother's issues, as well as his anger and confusion resulting from being over-bonded with her, set him up for a sexual trap. This pattern is very common, but can take different forms. Simplified, it looks like this. When a man and woman have a balanced marriage there is an emotional/sexual loop between them.

Both give emotionally and sexually, sometimes men less emotionally and women less sexually. But when a man's emotional support of his wife is lacking, she begins to look to another person for primary emotional support. Most often she finds this in a relationship with her mother or with her son. The rule of thumb is that it is the youngest or the weakest son that she will bond with if there is more than one boy in the family. This happens either from lack of awareness, or because the husband does not believe he can be truthful because she is unwilling to hear his feelings.

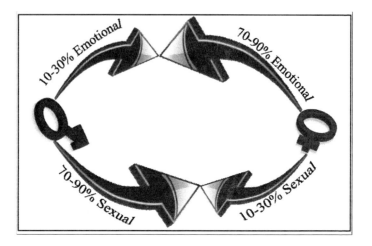

Here is one of the core issues of how men make women crazy. Man and woman together make up the reflection of Love.[1] Men reflect the strength and integrity of Love and woman reflect the beauty and intuition of Love. The four parts are required for there to be wholeness in the marriage.

Anytime the husband is not strong enough to be totally honest, his integrity breaks, thus the foundation for his wife's beauty and intuition breaks down and she starts to feel crazy. She brings up her concerns and he seals the deal with, "You're crazy! I would never hold anything back from you, and I am not attracted to that woman" basically telling her what she wants to hear and locking her into not asking anymore about whatever topic is now off-limits because she is "crazy" to bring it up.

Fundamentally boyfriends, fiancé's and husbands make their women crazy by not being honest with them, then telling them that their intuition is wrong. Why do men do this? Two reasons: First they often do not feel good enough or worthy because they don't have a finish line. And secondly, men often have insecurity about themselves that is difficult to recognize.

Therefore they are vulnerable to finding comfort however they can. The worst comfort for a relationship is another woman, who feeds his ego. But that is not the only comfort that seduces men. The list is long: drugs, alcohol, computer games, work, hobbies, care of parents' needs, children, friends, church work, etc. Notice that most of these are not wrong in-and-of-themselves, but it is the drawing of primary comfort from them that breaks down the system of a man being able to share his strength and integrity.

Twist of the Dagger!
Enter fear. A man's fear that his significant other will not approve of the time, or energy he spends getting that other approval— approval being a core addiction—he hides. He is hiding because he fears being disapproved of.[2]

Notice the twist; it is not disapproval that is the problem but the fear of the disapproval. This is where the agreements about feelings become critical. In order to establish a safe relationship where it is okay for a man to share his temptations, hurts, and behaviors, the woman has to allow those things to be heard. It has to be okay for a man to share things that may hurt his woman. If the fear of disapproval is present, it will be a barrier to intimacy.

Defusing this fear does not happen all at once. A couple has to begin with agreeing with the rules about feelings that we went over in Chapter 2. Then demonstrate that with honest sharing. Forgiveness becomes critical, because the dagger scars on our hearts are going to hurt when we start using the key. Fear of disapproval is real, and does not go away without painful work.

Most of the time there are hurts between a couple that require much forgiveness, understanding of the pain, and boundaries that are difficult to keep. It is not easy, but it is so worth it. When I (Jami) hear Marla say "I would go through it all again to be where we are together now," it nearly breaks my heart with joy. I find it almost unbelievable that she could forgive my betrayal[3] and be willing to go through the rejection or her family, the difficult process of recovery, the loss of money and standing in the community, and much more, to be here now.

Yet we find this is true of most everyone committed to a relationship. Even if they say, as Marla did, that they would never forgive an affair, they most often do. The depth of grace written into our very DNA is a true reflection of the Love that created us. Together we are a mirror of Love's strength, integrity, beauty and intuition. That is, if we allow Love to flow through us.

---

[1] Stasi Eldredge's book *Captivating* explores this concept in more detail.

[2] See Dr. Joyce Myers *Approval Addiction* book.

[3] See our book *Our Real Journey*. You can purchase it at www.inviteinc. org.

FIFTEEN

What is strength and integrity?

One of the most devastating issues in our culture today is answering the question "What does it take to be a man?" In a world dominated by millionaire athletes being arrested, and pictures of "tough guys" in expensive cars with flashy women, how does an average boy become a true man of strength and integrity?

There is a huge need for mentors who have balance in their lives. We must build small communities that value honesty with feelings. This demonstrates the values of love and faith with strength. It is only by sharing core feelings clearly that a boy can become a man. Doing this without fear creates the integrity that becomes the foundation for a woman to share her beauty and intuition safely.

We are grateful to our fathers who were able to give us a better life than they had. We particularly appreciate Marla's dad, Jerry. He has gone the extra mile and learned forgiveness for his own life. He has made a priority of expressing feelings to not only his wife but his children and grandchildren. This allows for beauty to flourish around him. And this makes for the foundation of community.

We need a multi-generational community where the seniors are committed to more than the status quo. Where they choose to mentor younger men into warriors, kings and sages instead of sitting back and "retiring."[1] This is one of the key ingredients for healing the cuts from the daggers of life – a multi-generational community of people growing in a healing process.

Beauty and Intuition Realized

It is so difficult for a woman to truly feel beautiful as well as valued for her intuition. I (Marla) know this to be true in my life. As women, our beauty has been attacked since the Garden of Eden. From the Genesis account of creation, Eve and her beauty were the crowning achievement. And ever since then the Devil has been attacking women in their most vulnerable place – their beauty.

Look around and you will see signs of this everywhere. In the mailbox you'll find the clothing catalog with the half-dressed, voluptuous blond; on the billboard you'll see the images of sexy woman holding beers; on television you'll experience sexual prowess from women that would never been allowed 20 years ago. These images create in my heart, and the hearts of women around the world, the overriding fear that I will never be enough.

My beauty is not the beauty the world is looking for.[2]

But this is a lie! As Jami and I have grown spiritually and moved into deeper intimacy, and as Jami has become a powerful man of strength and integrity I have grown to believe in my beauty and intuition.

I know that I am beautiful and that my intuition is spot-on because of the connection Jami and I have with true Love. Jami trusts me when I express to him that I feel someone is "unsafe", and does not ever cause me to feel like I am crazy for having these intuitions. It has taken several years and the rebuilding of trust and confidence, but my Higher Power has given me the amazing knowledge that I am worthy of love; that I am loved, visible and beautiful. Wow.

Watching a woman come in to her beauty and intuition is incredible. We have seen it happen over and over again. But one particular woman has gone all the way, and has recently discovered true love and intimacy because of it. Her name is Jennifer, and here is her story.

Our first coaching session with Jennifer and Kevin was just about to begin. Glancing out the window I saw a handsome young couple stepping out of an upscale vehicle. Jennifer looked very familiar. She was the twin sister of Gina, whom we had met just weeks earlier while we were handing out brochures for our coaching practice to local businesses. And that was how Jennifer had heard about what we do for couples.

As their story unfolded before us, we became increasingly hopeful that their marriage could be saved. After a few sessions we decided that maybe an entire week of intensive coaching daily would be effective and allow Kevin to open up and get in touch with the core pain that he seemed to be holding on to.

It was awesome to watch Jennifer move from fairly compulsive and controlling to a humble, graceful woman seemingly overnight as each layer of the onion peeled off for her on her journey to forgiveness. She was all in, and taking full responsibility for holding on to unforgiveness of Kevin for something that had taken place while they were engaged. She was feeling excited about the love for Kevin that was returning in powerful ways.

But she was also struggling with the feeling that something just wasn't "right" and that Kevin wasn't being completely truthful. When she confronted him with the idea that maybe he was having a relationship with another woman, he lashed out at her angrily and told her that was just "crazy."

Kevin had stated that if Jennifer could forgive him for "that one thing"—the event that took place during their engagement—it would allow his heart to be turned back to her. Apparently, he had not been truthful. Or maybe it was his desire, but he couldn't let go of one little thing. And he wouldn't tell us what that one thing was for several sessions. Finally the whole truth was laid out on the table. Kevin revealed that he was having an affair and was unwilling to let this other woman go.

No matter what Jennifer said or did, and no matter how often we expressed that their marriage could make it through this and that they could actually have a stronger relationship than ever, Kevin was resolute. He had made up his mind to leave Jennifer and their 3 year old daughter, Kelly, and pursue this other relationship. Remember Jennifer's intuition that something wasn't right? It had been exactly right, and Kevin had caused her to feel guilty, or "crazy", for not believing him when he said there wasn't another woman.

Kevin moved out that week. But for Jennifer this catapulted her to incredible personal and spiritual growth. She continued coaching with us, and discovered that she had allowed her perfectionism to control her life and she was ready to be released from it. She also chose to listen to our counsel and pursue a deeper relationship with intimate Love through focused journaling and reading empowering books. She remains the very best coaching client we have ever had. Each week she'd go home with new homework, and she would return with her homework done and always had amazing insights. We kept telling her that if she continued on this path of growth she would someday find a man with strength and integrity who would treasure her heart and allow her beauty and intuition to shine through. No intimidation, no power struggles, no abandonment, just powerful love and peace.

Jennifer also became one of our best friends. Yes, this is an uncommon occurrence within the world of "counseling", but we are coaches not counselors. We often become great friends with our clients because we are on this journey together. We share our story with them as much as they share theirs' with us. Our goal is to direct and guide, as a coach on the football field would do with his players. We have been blessed with a method to share the forgiveness and healing journey that saved our marriage, and our lives, with others. And when someone like Jennifer comes into our life we are amazed at what Love does for them, and for us in the process.

And the coolest part of this story is that just this week Jennifer became engaged to the love of her life. He is the man we told her she would find; one with strength and integrity who treasures Jennifer's heart and allows her beauty and intuition to shine through. She no longer doubts that she is worthy of love. She no longer clings to perfectionism and control so that her life is "safe". She allows Love to guide her, and she allows her fiancé to love her. He trusts her intuition and listens to her, allowing her to never feel crazy or uncertain.[3] And this is possible for you, the reader, right now, right here, today.

---

[1] John Eldredge in his book *The Way of the Wild Heart* explores this concept in detail.

[2] Stasi Eldredge's book *Captivating* explores this concept in more detail.

[3] Note: Jennifer and Kip were married March 20, 2010 – by all accounts he is everything Jennifer ever wanted.

SIXTEEN

Traps for Strength and Beauty

> *"Waiting is a trap. There will always be reasons to wait. The truth is, there are only two things in life, reasons and results, and reasons simply don't count."*

Dr. Robert Anthony

> *"Your story is vital and part of a much larger story but it means nothing without the core feelings."*

Marla and Jami

It is a battle to grow in your innate giftedness. No one would go out to battle on their own, or keep their weaknesses to themselves. What is obvious suicide is often attempted out of pride or self-promotion. Hurt feelings that are not expressed can cripple the strongest looking warrior. Napoleon was defeated at Waterloo probably because he ignored an ulcer, it bled through and his generals were afraid to confront him about inaction on the battlefield while he was sitting nearly unconscious. He was defeated with nearly ten-thousand elite troops in reserve.

Temptation is all around us flirting with us and telling us that a little self indulgence won't hurt anyone. Pretending is the most dangerous pitfall. Pretending that we are not tempted; pretending that we would never be attracted to "those" kinds of behavior. Just put in the flavor of your temptation. Pride, sexuality, envy, greed, power… the list is long. But the remedy is simple. Not easy but simple. It may be the most difficult thing you ever do, but it is not complex. Follow the four steps we offer here: 1) Listen and express feelings; 2) Offer forgiveness; 3) Vision future intimacy; and, 4) Enter into strength and beauty.

Twist of the dagger

"We tried this and it isn't working." We have never had anyone say this and be true. In our coaching we ask people for three basic things that make the four things above possible: Journal daily including a short "worthy" statement, check-in daily, and write six forgiveness letters. Without fail when things are not working they will say "we have been doing what you say and we still fight." The next question is can you show me your journal with daily entries? Worthy statement? Do you check-in every day? If the answer is no, there is no wonder why you still have difficulty??

We understand change is hard. But it is much more painful to stay the same. Coach Peterson of our beloved Boise State Bronco Football program says, "You are either getting better, or worse." We agree. That is a fact for football teams, marriages and individuals.

The cost of not improving your marriage is more than we can measure. The impact on your personal lives is staggering by itself. Add in the hurt for your children, extended family, and community around you and it is multiplied hundreds of times.

In our experience anyone can do anything if their reason is big enough. When someone doesn't want to take the time to do just three basics they either don't care, don't understand or they just won't take the time to care and understand. Sometimes "Don't" and "Won't" are the same thing.

We are about saving relationships and building intimacy. We believe firmly that if we can make it through the muck and pain in our relationship, anyone can. We started helping people through a domestic violence program and watched some very nasty situations transform. Admittedly the odds are slim when violence is part of the scene. But if both parties are willing to be accountable while doing the work above ANYTHING is possible.

SEVENTEEN

Transforming Your Strength and Beauty

> *"A radical inner transformation and rise to a new level of consciousness might be the only real hope we have in the current global crisis brought on by the dominance of the Western mechanistic paradigm."*
>
> Stanislav Grof

> *"Change is hard, but staying where you are is worse!"*
>
> Marla and Jami

How do men make women crazy? The same way women make men crazy; through sabotaging intuition. *When you know something is wrong in your heart, but choose to believe it is really okay, it makes you crazy.* It may not always be intentional; in fact, most often it is done out of fear. Ironically, it is done out of the fear that the truth may be painful for you. But regardless of the reason it usually begins with a statement from your spouse that invalidates your intuition regardless of whether you are a man or woman. And he or she calls you "crazy". Like what I told Marla, "I would never dream of getting together with that woman! That is crazy talk."

The sabotage is often compounded if we get a mixed message from our opposite sex parent before and/or after marriage, and then make our spouse responsible for resolving it. The sabotage is almost always in the area of *strength* for men and *beauty* for women.

We know that there is a war over your heart. If evil can cripple your capacity for intimacy it wins. So it works very hard on hurting us early in life so that we will not trust, or grow in our strength and beauty. But Love travels all roads to heal our hearts. Love calls us to know true intimacy.

Because of this, we have within us more than enough strength and beauty. One person can make enough of an impact to completely change a relationship, a family and a community. Veronica was one such person. She was in a twenty plus year relationship and hated her husband. The relationship was unhealthy and abusive.

She began our process with one motivation – to get out of her depression. She was going to get out one way or another, and the only thing that had stopped her from committing suicide was her children. But even they were not enough any longer. Cheating on her husband just made her feel worse. The separation and the violence between them kept growing, and she had drawn her children into her lies and leaned on them for far too much support.

She began with the focused journaling, starting each day by reading an empowering book and writing out the five parts of the journaling process and a simple affirmation: "I am worthy of being a beautiful woman". This is critical to changing bad thinking. The bad thinking is the thoughts that we all have that we are not good enough. These are not our thoughts in the beginning. They are often the criticism we experienced from our parents and they can be crippling. Unfortunately, the way we think becomes a habit that is built into our brains by synapses that are glued together more firmly every time we repeat a thought. Suddenly "I am a bad person" becomes hard-wired into us, even though it is a lie.

For Veronica the message was clear — "make everyone else happy or you will get yelled at, even if they are abusing you." When she told her parents she was being sexually abused by both her brothers, she was invalidated and told that she was lying and that she was bad. So began the forgiveness process. Writing letters to her parents revealed even more hurt, anger and frustration. But in forgiving them, and beginning to develop boundaries, she started feeling hopeful, if not for her relationship at least for putting one foot in front the other.

Writing the letters back to herself revealed that she had never dreamed that anyone would ever affirm her. She led a self-fulfilling prophesy in this by cutting short any conversation that might lift her up. Day by day she was able to get forgiveness into her heart for her entire family of origin and then her children, husband, the church, God and herself. It was the most difficult thing she had ever done but she was able to stop her dysfunctional thinking process because of the forgiveness growing in her heart. It was not easy and, as she was reminded several times by her children of the commitment to have safe boundaries with them, it even made her angry.

But anger is good, and she took the energy of her anger and used it to express herself. The depression began to lift. Her eyes began to brighten and her beauty began to shine more, and in ways she did not expect. Options became more visible to her, and surprising herself, she began to take advantage of them.

She was then able to join a woman's group and share her pain with them. This was something she would have never done without a solid prayer life to silence the shaming voices in her head, and forgiveness in her heart. And as she participated she found something else that surprised her — she had something to offer. Her deep wounds, as well as years of feeling like a broken person that had been thrown in life's trash, had given her insight and empathy for others that had low self-esteem and pain. Sometimes our dreams have to be shattered before we can see the bigger dream that Love has for us.

Veronica's husband started seeing her beauty more as well. The fact that she would not engage in his passive control techniques caused him to wake up. He started his own investigation, and began our process for himself. He healed and took on the responsibility of leading their family forward with his strength and integrity. Finally, one day, she found herself looking at her husband and saying "I am attracted to him again!" They began to re-court and he publicly asked her to remarry him. While there are still effects of years lost, the future is bright and they are beginning to serve in our community. Their service is bringing to them a very high level of satisfaction!

There is no accident with the order of events here. We all have hurts, but when we ask to be healed we are brought into an intimate relationship. Grace and forgiveness begin to become a strong part of our character. We begin to serve others, getting out of our narcissistic habits. And as we do so, we find a new dream and a bigger dream than we ever thought possible. Then we begin to live fully in that dream.

The stories we tell in this book are true and prove that Love is bigger than any disaster that might be in your life. They are as shocking as our story. You can read more about our story in the book entitled *Our Real Journey*, and it also supports our belief that any relationship can be saved, invigorated and that it will grow for an eternity. It is not easy, but it *is* worth it. It requires daily focused journaling, a commitment to forgiveness, learning good boundaries and expressing yourself fully and safely in a community where you begin to serve with a high level of satisfaction. There are no shortcuts. We have tried many of them and failed. But if you are able to be committed to a relationship and follow these simple steps with the hard work it takes to complete them consistently, anything is possible.

It has been in our lives. We would go through it all again to be where we are today. Join us on this journey and see for yourself what is possible in our life. You can be filled with Love. **You are strong and beautiful, no matter who you are and where you have been.**

EPILOGUE

Please take what you can from what we offer here and keep on the journey you have started. We welcome your feedback and questions. It actually inspires us to adjust and grow in our process. It is our privilege to share with you, and our highest hopes are for more intimacy and satisfaction in your life. We hold a unique belief that your primary relationship should grow more intimate every day. People will try and tell you that this is a hopeless quest, and you will be tempted to give up, but we know it is possible because we are experiencing it even now—FAR more intimacy than we had ever even dreamed about. Don't give up. Don't give in. Focus on the bright spots, and know that you are never alone!

Thank you for taking the time to read our book. We hope to meet you and hear what it is that you are doing with all that you have learned.

HEALING ACTIVITIES

Discovering Your Core Fear from "The DNA of Relationships"
Gary Smalley

#1 Conflict Identification

- Think about a recent conflict that really hurt you or made you angry.

- Identify more specifically how you were feeling at the time.

- Fill in the blank in the following sentence: "If only you would stop saying or doing _____ I would not be so upset."

#2 From the following list, what emotions were you feeling at the time of the conflict (*the three most important*):

___ Unsure	___ Uncomfortable	___ Frightened
___ Apathetic	___ Confused	___ Anxious
___ Puzzled	___ Worried	___ Horrified
___ Upset	___ Disgusted	___ Disturbed
___ Sullen	___ Resentful	___ Furious
___ Sad	___ Bitter	___ Other: _____
___ Hurt	___ Fed up	___ Other: _____
___Frustrated	___ Disappointed	___ Other: _____
___ Wearied	___ Miserable	

____ Torn up   ____ Guilty

____ Shamed   ____ Embarrassed

#3 Identifying Your Fear
"As a result of the conflict I felt . . ."

____ Rejected	____ Abandoned	____ Crazy
____ Disconnected	____ Like a Failure	____ Helpless
____ Defective	____ Inadequate	____ Inferior
____ Inferior	____ Invalidated	____ Unloved
____ Dissatisfied	____ Cheated	____ Worthless
____ Unaccepted	____ Judged	____ Humiliated
____ Ignored	____ Insignificant	____ Other: _____

#4 Identify your reactions:
What do you feel when you <u>(insert the most important feeling from previous page)</u>? How do you react when you feel that way?

#5 List three main feelings from #3:

•   Core Fear #1 _____
•   Core Fear #2 _____
•   Core Fear #3 _____
•

#6 List three main reactions from #4 when someone pushes your core fear button:

•   Reaction #1 _____
•   Reaction #2 _____
•   Reaction #3 _____

Your response to these exercises should help you understand your part in the Key-Dagger: your core fear button and your reaction.

Remember that it's very common for your reactions to push the core fear button of the other person in the conflict.

Going Through Your Childhood House
Jami and Marla Keller

Picture yourself in your childhood home of your earliest memories. Think about the rooms. Who's in your house? Which rooms are they in? What are they doing? When I (Marla) did this in counseling, I discovered that my house was empty. Finally when I conjured up someone in my home it was my mom. She was in the kitchen cooking. When I attempted to get her attention, she turned and paid attention for two seconds then went back to cooking.

This exercise helped me understand that I felt totally alone and abandoned in my childhood. My mom was there, but not really present. Try this and share it with you spouse or significant other. It is very enlightening.

Check-In
Jami and Marla Keller
Check-in is the Key to your lover's heart. Learn this and the world will open up for you and life will take on new meaning and power. The most important thing to remember about expressing feelings is to use the "I Message" which goes like this:

1. **When** – Describe the person's behavior you are reacting to in a non-blaming and non-judgmental manner. This can also be a positive thing that you are appreciating your spouse for. It's not always negative.

2. **The effects are** – Describe the obvious or tangible effects of that behavior because your partner will benefit from knowing what your reaction to the

behavior was. This will allow them to understand you more fully.

3. **I feel** – Express specific feeling from the *Feeling Wheel*. Remember, this is more important than the story. This also allows your partner to see that you are taking responsibility for your own feelings.

4. **I'd prefer *OR* my boundary is *OR* I appreciate you for** – Let your partner know what you would prefer to happen. Be careful about boundaries because when you state one you need to be certain that you will keep it, otherwise it will not be effective.

Be careful to not discount someone else's feelings. Their feelings are real for them. Their perceptions are their reality. And it's okay because you are not responsible for their feelings, but you do love the other person and desire to understand and have empathy for their feelings.